GERMAN ANTIGUERRILLA OPERATIONS IN THE BALKANS
(1941–1944)

FOREWORD

The purpose of this study is to describe briefly the German campaign against the guerrillas in the Balkans during the period of the European Axis occupation, from the end of hostilities against Greece and Yugoslavia in April 1941 to the capture of Belgrade by the Soviet forces and the Partisans in October 1944. The activities of Germany's Italian, Bulgarian, Croatian, and other allies, as well as the British, Soviet, and United States forces in the area, are treated only to the extent that they affected German operations. In sequence of time, this study is a continuation of Department of the Army CMH Pub 104-18, The German Campaigns in the Balkans (Spring 1941), of November 1953.

The material for this study was obtained from German military records now in the custody of The Adjutant General, Department of the Army. In addition to these official records, monographs by former German officers who participated in these operations furnished considerable general information and were of assistance in supplementing the terse official reports of specific actions. The authors of these monographs, prepared for the Historical Division, United States Army, Europe, include General der Gebirgstruppen (Lieutenant General) Hubert Lanz, former commander of the XXII Mountain Corps, and Polizeioberst (Colonel of Police) Karl Gaisser, German technical adviser to the Croatian Police.

The work of preparing this study was done by Major Robert M. Kennedy of the Office of the Chief of Military History. In its presentation, every effort was made to give an accurate account of the protracted attempt by the German occupation forces to destroy their elusive guerrilla enemy in this secondary theater of war from 1941 through 1944.

CONTENTS

	Page
Part One. THE BALKAN AREA AND ITS PEOPLES	1

Chapter 1. Physical Geography

I. Topography	2
II. Climate	3

2. National States

I. General	4
II. Greece	4
III. Yugoslavia	5
IV. Albania	6
V. Bulgaria, Hungary, Romania, and Turkey	7

3. Transportation and Communications

I. General	8
II. Main Rail Lines	8
III. Principal Highways	9
IV. Waterways, Airfields, and Signal Facilities	9

Part Two. THE OCCUPATION OF THE BALKANS AND THE RISE OF THE GUERRILLA MOVEMENT (1941–42)	10

Chapter 4. The Occupation Zones and Forces

I. Division and Dismemberment	13
II. The Italians	13
III. The Germans	15
IV. The Bulgarians and Hungarians	17
V. The Puppet Governments	18

5. The Early Movement and Axis Countermeasures

I. Yugoslavia	20
II. Greece	27

6. Organization of Guerrilla Units

I. Unit and Command Structure	31
II. Communications and Supply	32
III. Training and Tactics	33

Part Three. THE GUERRILLA MOVEMENT IN GREECE, YUGOSLAVIA, AND ALBANIA (1943–44)	35

Chapter 7. Operations (January–August 1943)

I. Yugoslavia	36
II. Greece	38
III. The German Situation by Mid-1943	40

8. The Defection of Italy and Its Effects

I. General	44
II. Yugoslavia and Albania	44
III. Greece	45

CONTENTS

Part Three. THE GUERRILLA MOVEMENT IN GREECE, YUGOSLAVIA, AND ALBANIA (1943–44)—Continued

Page

Chapter 9. Operations to the End of 1943

    I. General 47
    II. Yugoslavia and Albania 50
    III. Greece 52

10. Operations in 1944

    I. General 53
    II. The Area of Army Group E 54
    III. The Area of Army Group F 64

11. GEMSBOCK and STEINADLER 70

Part Four. RESULTS AND CONCLUSIONS 73

Appendix I. Chronology of Events 79
    II. Bibliographical Note 82

MAPS

No.
1. General Reference Map .... Facing 1
2. The Partition of Greece 12
3. The Partition of Yugoslavia 14
4. German Dispositions in the Balkans as of Mid-August 1944 .... Facing 53
5. German Estimate of Guerrilla Strength and Dispositions in Greece as of Mid-August 1944 61
6. German Estimate of Guerrilla Strength and Dispositions in Yugoslavia and Albania as of Mid-August 1944 .... Facing 67
7. Operation GEMSBOCK .... Facing 70
8. Operation STEINADLER .... Facing 72

CHARTS

No.
1. German Ground Forces in Occupied Greece and Yugoslavia as of July 1941 17
2. German Ground Forces in Occupied Greece and Yugoslavia as of 1 December 1942 27
3. German and Bulgarian Ground Forces in Occupied Greece, Yugoslavia and Albania as of 26 December 1943 51
4. German Ground Forces in Occupied Yugoslavia and Albania as of the Fall of Belgrade 20 October 1944 68

PART ONE

THE BALKAN AREA AND ITS PEOPLES

The term "Balkan" is derived from a Turkish word meaning "mountain." As used by the English-speaking nations, however, the word refers to that peninsula of southeastern Europe lying between the Black and Adriatic Seas and extending south to the Mediterranean. To the north, the geographic boundary is less definite, but is generally accepted as the area south of the line of the Danube and Sava, west along the Kupa River, whence an imaginary line is drawn to the Adriatic port of Fiume.

From north to south, the broad expanse of the Danube Basin gives way to the mountain ranges of Yugoslavia and Bulgaria. The remainder of the peninsula consists mainly of rugged mountains, broken occasionally by such features as the coastal lowlands of Albania, the area surrounding the Gulf of Salonika in Greece, and the lowlands of Turkish Thrace.

The Balkan peoples have been in contact with the inhabitants of Asia Minor, the Hungarian Plain, Central Europe, and the highly developed Mediterranean civilizations for thousands of years. Nevertheless it is still possible to distinguish such ethnic groupings as the Albanians, Serbs, Bulgars, Turks, Greeks, and Vlachs, the last a seminomadic race of herdsmen being absorbed gradually into the various national states into which the Balkan area is divided.

Occupied for centuries by Romans, Turks, Austrians, and Hungarians, the Balkan peoples were forced to adopt the methods of irregular warfare in the struggle against their oppressors. When not resisting foreign invaders, they battled one another or kept alive their fighting traditions in bitter blood feuds. The mountainous terrain of their peninsula, with few good roads or rail lines, hampered the countermeasures of regular forces and made possible sustained guerrilla operations.

CHAPTER 1
PHYSICAL GEOGRAPHY

1. Topography

The most important physical feature of the Balkans as a scene of military operations is its wild terrain. The brushy mountain country, craggy peaks, and roadless forest areas offer irregular troops numerous places to hide, opportunity to shift forces unseen even from the air, and locations for ambush.

To the west, the Dinaric Alps follow Yugoslavia's Adriatic coast in a southeasterly direction and bar access to the interior of the country. Although some coastal areas are fertile, the limestone composition of these mountains makes the hinterland a barren region incapable of supporting any considerable population. Deep gorges make transverse movement difficult, and there are only a few secondary roads and rail lines until the central Yugoslav uplands to the east are reached.

From the headwaters of the Drin River, the length of Albania to the port city of Valona, the mountains draw back from the coast, making for easier access to the interior, and assume a north-south direction. South of Valona, the mountains resume their southeasterly march and merge into the Greek Pindus. These latter extend to the Gulf of Corinth, reappearing on the southern side of the gulf in the Peloponnesus.

Directly south of Greece proper is the large island of Crete, of considerable strategic importance. Other Greek islands dotting the Ionian and Aegean Seas are Corfu, Cephalonia, Zante, Rhodes, the Dodecanese, the Sporades, the Cyclades, Lemnos, and Khios.

The central uplands, east of the mountain chain extending the length of the Balkan Peninsula, are fertile enough to support large centers of population and some industry. To the north, this region is drained by the Sava and Morava Rivers, flowing into the Danube; to the south, by the Vardar, wending its way through Macedonia to the Gulf of Salonika and the Aegean.

The eastern portion of the peninsula is bisected by the Balkan Mountains. To the north this area descends to the Danubian plain; to the south, to the steppe-like lands of Turkish Thrace.

II. Climate

With the exception of its coastal areas, the Balkan Peninsula has a central European climate, characterized by warm and rainy summers and cold winters, differing little from the Danubian lands to the north. The Dalmatian coast of Yugoslavia, facing the Adriatic, and the Ionian and western Aegean coasts of Greece enjoy variations of the Mediterranean type of climate, with warm, dry summers and mild, rainy winter seasons; other coastal areas have a climate between that of central Europe and the Mediterranean—for example, the north Aegean coast with its hot summers and cold winters and the Black Sea coast with its moderately hot summers and cold winters.

CHAPTER 2

NATIONAL STATES

I. General

The peace treaties following the Balkan Wars of 1912 and 1913, World War I, and the Greek-Turkish conflict ending in 1923 resolved the frontiers of the various Balkan states until 1939. In that year, Italy occupied Albania and proceeded to implement her designs for dominating the Balkan Peninsula.

The creation of these states had satisfied many national aspirations, but numerous minority and territorial problems were left unsettled, and both Italians and Germans were able to turn them to their own advantage. Among the dissatisfied were the Hungarians in the part of north central Yugoslavia that had once been part of the Austro-Hungarian Empire; the Italians along Yugoslavia's northwestern border; the Macedonians, torn among the Bulgarians, Yugoslavs, and Greeks; and the large colonies of Austrians and Germans in northern Yugoslavia. There were also bitter rivalries between member nations of the same state, as the Serbs and Croats of Yugoslavia, and both Yugoslavia and Bulgaria were resentful of Greek possession of the Aegean coast. Despite the efforts of some Balkan leaders to foster intra-Balkan cooperation and good will prior to 1941, these sources of animosity and friction remained to hamper resistance to Italian and German subjugation.

II. Greece

Slightly smaller in area than England, Greece had a population of less than eight million in 1941. Migrations and exchanges of population, chief among them the replacement of Turks in western Thrace with a million and a quarter Greeks expelled from Asia Minor in 1922-24, contributed to making the inhabitants of the Hellenic state predominantly Greek by the outbreak of World War II. Although there were a number of Albanians and Vlachs in the Pindus Mountains area, they presented no minority problem.

Athens, the capital, with its port city of Piraeus, was the nucleus of the Greek maritime system; Salonika was a center of land transportation and an important seaport for the more northerly of the Balkan countries. With an economy based chiefly on ocean commerce and agriculture, Greece had no heavy industry. Rather, it restricted its processing of goods mainly to olive oil, currants, and tobacco. Cereals led among heavy food imports, since Greece could not feed its own population on its domestic production.

When Italian forces attacked from occupied Albania on 28 October 1940, the Greeks adopted a strategy of holding lightly on their left, allowing Italian columns to advance deep into the barren Pindus, while they resisted strongly and then launched a counteroffensive on their right. Their advance brought the Greeks into Albania, where they presented a serious threat to the left flank of the Italian forces to the south.

Despite their victories over the Italian invaders, the Greeks could not long resist the fast-moving German forces that intervened in the Greek-Italian conflict on 6 April 1941. Greece surrendered to the Germans on 23 April, and was then required to surrender to the Italians as well. This submission to an enemy they had all but defeated aroused the resentment of the Greeks. Later coupled with the occupation of most of Greece by Italian forces, it contributed in no small measure to the rise of the Greek resistance movement.

III. Yugoslavia

A most heterogeneous state, the homeland of the Serbs, Croats, and Slovenes, derived its name from the Slavic terms for South Slav and became a state following World War I. Yugoslavia had a population of nearly sixteen millions by 1941, and in geographic area was slightly smaller than the state of Wyoming. Almost one half of its inhabitants, or six and one-half million people, were Serbs, occupying the areas of the former Kingdom of Serbia and the old provinces of Bosnia, Hercegovina, and Dalmatia. The Serbs used the Cyrillic alphabet, professed mainly the Orthodox faith though many Serbs were Moslems, and stubbornly resisted the Central Powers in World War I. Serbian Belgrade was the seat of the Yugoslav national government, lending credence to the claim of the minorities that the Serbs dominated the state. It was the Serbs' violent protest to Regent Paul's accord with Hitler and their overthrow of the government in March 1941 that precipitated the German attack the following month, and it was from among the Serbs that the Chetniks rose to resist the occupation forces.

Next in numbers to the Serbs were the Croats, some three and three-quarter million, inhabiting the northwestern part of Yugoslavia. The traditional capital of the Croats was Zagreb, and their territory was part of the Austro-Hungarian Empire until the end of World War I. The Croats were culturally more advanced than the Serbs, were western European in their outlook, and the majority professed Catholicism. Although their language was related closely to that of the Serbs, the Croats used the Latin alphabet. German influence among the Croats in the pre-1941 period was strong, and it was on the traditional Croatian hostility to the Serbs that the invaders placed much confidence in 1941.

Last among the major racial groups comprising the Yugoslav state were the Slovenes, inhabiting the most northerly portion of the country and numbering some one and one-half million. Like the Croats, the Slovenes were culturally well advanced, used the Latin alphabet, were oriented toward the West, and for the most part Catholic. Their historic capital was Ljubljana, and the German influence was very marked.

Smaller national minorities included one-half million Hungarians and almost as many Albanians; one-quarter million Romanians; and splinter groups of Czechs, Slovaks, and other Slavic peoples. There were also well over one-half million Austrians and Germans.

In 1941 over three quarters of the Yugoslav population worked the land, and agriculture formed the nation's economic base. The chief exports were lumber, bauxite, copper, some iron ore, and processed fruits; imports included textiles and machinery. Deposits of iron ore near the surface of the ground could not be used to build up a sizable steel industry because of the shortage of coking coal.

The German onslaught of 6 April 1941 caught the Yugoslavs in the midst of general mobilization, a measure that had been delayed to avoid giving provocation to Hitler. A devastating air attack on Belgrade the day hostilities commenced crippled communications between the Yugoslav High Command and the armies in the field. To placate the dissatisfied minorities, which charged that the Serb-dominated government would defend only Serb-inhabited areas, the Yugoslav Army was deployed all around the borders of the country. To make the Yugoslav position even more difficult, thousands of Croat reservists did not report as directed for military service. By 17 April the German Second Army from the northwest and the Twelfth Army from the southeast, assisted to some extent by their Italian allies, had broken through the thin shell of resistance around the country, captured all major cities, and forced the Yugoslav High Command to capitulate.

IV. Albania

This smallest of the Balkan countries, approximately the size of Maryland, had a population of slightly over one million in 1941. After centuries of Turkish domination, Albania had declared its independence in 1912, but it was not until the end of World War I that the tiny state could consider itself free of its stronger neighbors.

Consisting mainly of Gheg tribesmen in the north and Tosks in the south, the Albanians were almost exclusively an agricultural and stock-raising people. Mineral and lumber resources were largely undeveloped because of a lack of transportation, although the Italians managed to produce some oil and completed part of the short rail line from Tirana to the Adriatic after their occupation of the country in 1939.

In normal times, Albania exported quantities of wool, dairy products, tobacco, hides, and some cattle. Textiles and other finished products led among imports.

Exploited by the Italians, Albania furnished 12,000 auxiliaries to Mussolini's disastrous campaign against Greece in 1940. A large number of these, however, promptly deserted. In the rugged mountain areas of Albania, Italian control was little more than nominal, and the occupation garrisons usually restricted themselves to the few towns, to the through roads, and to the coastal regions.

V. Bulgaria, Hungary, Romania, and Turkey

Since Bulgaria, Romania, and Hungary succumbed to German pressure to become partners of the European Axis, and Turkey remained neutral until the end of World War II, this study will consider these countries but briefly.

Bulgaria, approximately the size of Ohio, had a population of a little more than seven million in 1941. Ethnically close to the Russians, the language of the Bulgarians was Slavonic. With an economy primarily agricultural, the chief Bulgarian exports were fruits and dairy products.

Hungary, not a true Balkan country but adjacent to the Balkan area and continually involved in its problems, had a population of slightly over nine million and was approximately the size of Indiana. The economy of Hungary was agricultural, with meat and cereals the chief exports.

Romania, also outside the Balkan area proper, was approximately the size of Oregon, and had a population of fifteen and one-half million, three quarters of whom were engaged in agriculture. With its rich Ploesti fields, Romania was the largest oil producer in the Balkan-Danubian area.

Turkey, as large as Texas and Maine combined, had a population of nineteen and one half million and an agricultural economy in 1941. In the Balkans proper, Turkey had only a few thousand square miles in eastern Thrace.

CHAPTER 3

TRANSPORTATION AND COMMUNICATIONS

I. General

The rugged terrain of the Balkans proper has been a heavy handicap to the development of an adequate transportation and communication net, and the frequent wars and changes in the political frontiers within the area have made the extension and improvement of facilities even more difficult. Such rail construction as could be compared favorably to that of western Europe in 1941 was restricted to the international lines connecting the capital cities and some lines in the lowland regions in the north.

Although the roads afforded somewhat more complete coverage than the rail lines, there were few hard-surface highways aside from those paralleling the main railroads. The terrain made necessary numerous serpentines and bridges, and detours were often difficult or impossible. On the whole, road repair was very deficient.

Cables connecting the various Balkan capitals were laid before World War I, and some improvements were made during the period preceding the attack in 1941. However, little was done to establish a unified and efficient cable network throughout the Balkan countries.

To remain within the scope of this study, it will be necessary to limit consideration of the transportation and communication net to that of importance to the occupation forces and the irregulars arrayed against them.

II. Main Rail Lines

At the time German forces overran the Balkans, Yugoslavia had approximately 6,000 miles and Greece 1,700 miles of railroad lines; both countries used the standard European gauge. The most important lines were those converging on Zagreb from Austria, Italy, and Hungary; the line Zagreb-Belgrade-Nish; and the lines Nish-Sofiya, and Nish-Salonika-Athens. All were vital to the Italian-German war effort, since British air and naval activity made supply by sea difficult and the Germans did not have the necessary truck transport facilities. Too, in addition to the occupation forces, those units and installations supporting the German air and naval effort in the eastern Mediterranean had to be supplied by rail, along the line Zagreb-Belgrade-Nish-Salonika-Athens.

III. Principal Highways

The roads of Greece and Yugoslavia were poor, with the exception of a few international highways and limited areas in and about the capitals and major cities. Of the various road nets, the best were those in northwestern Yugoslavia, in the areas taken from the Austro-Hungarian Empire; about Belgrade; through Skoplje to Salonika; in the industrial area about Salonika; and in the Athens-Piraeus industrial and shipping complex.

To the German and Italian occupation forces, the most important road nets were those roughly paralleling the rail lines through northern Yugoslavia, including Belgrade; along the Vardar River to Salonika, thence along the Aegean coast to Athens; a system of roads through the northern half of the Peloponnesus; a series of secondary roads along the Adriatic coast of Yugoslavia; some tortuous roads through the Dinaric Alps; and a few main roads in western Greece. Though some of these roads were paved, the majority were built of crushed stone and unable to support sustained traffic and heavy trucks in any number without constant repair. In many places, lengths of paved road alternated with stretches of crushed stone.

IV. Waterways, Airfields, and Signal Facilities

While the Danube played a significant part in the logistical support of the attack forces, the waterways within Greece and Yugoslavia proper played little part in the later supply of the occupation troops. Perhaps that put to the most extensive use was the Corinth Canal, linking the Gulf of Corinth and the Aegean. By using this canal, the Italians were able to cut the distance from their supply bases along the Adriatic and Ionian Seas to Piraeus and Athens by some 130 miles, avoiding the open sea and British aircraft based in Egypt.

Airfield facilities in Greece and Yugoslavia, though not extensive, were more than adequate for the needs of the Germans and Italians. Stocks of gasoline and other supplies left behind in Greece by the British were put to use, and the slight damage to fighter bases was not enough to prevent their immediate utilization. Perhaps most important strategically were the excellent bases on Crete and in the Athens-Piraeus area.

Signal facilities in the various Balkan countries at the time of the occupation were incapable of supporting heavy traffic. Too, it was a simple matter for the guerrillas to disrupt the few long-distance cables and overhead wires that existed. The mountainous nature of the terrain circumscribed the use of radio, but it was on this and field telephone lines, plus liaison aircraft, that the occupation forces usually had to rely.

PART TWO

THE OCCUPATION OF THE BALKANS AND THE RISE OF THE GUERRILLA MOVEMENT (1941-42)

The German combat troops, scheduled to leave almost immediately to refit for Operation BARBAROSSA (the assault on the Soviet Union), had little time for prisoners after their quick conquest of Yugoslavia, and captured Greeks were paroled as a gesture of respect for their heroic effort in defense of their country. Thus, shortly after the cessation of hostilities, the Yugoslav and Greek forces were demobilized, their personnel idle, and stunned rather than crushed by their sudden defeat. Many had never seen the enemy, others had recently been on the offensive, as the Greek forces in Albania, and had been forced to stop fighting only when encircled by the Germans or because higher commanders had surrendered.

The German authorities were cognizant of the threat of these unemployed ex-soldiers and other dissident elements uniting to form a resistance movement. Moreover, the commencement of hostilities with the Soviet Union 2 months later made external support of such a movement most probable; aid by the Russians would serve to divert German divisions from the Russian theater of war, gain the Kremlin an opening wedge for the communization of the Balkans, and possibly even permit realization of the age-old Russian desire for access to the Adriatic and Mediterranean.

Little was done to forestall the obvious threat of revolt. Perhaps the Germans considered the few divisions they were leaving behind sufficient to secure Greece and Yugoslavia and keep up an uninterrupted flow of raw materials to the German war machine. Most certainly German planners were preoccupied with the approaching campaign against the Soviet Union. At any rate, German preparations to contain and destroy large-scale risings were inadequate. Belated German efforts as time passed succeeded only in quelling temporarily the growing surge of resistance in areas where the occupation authorities could mass superior forces. Suppression of the resistance movement became and remained for over 2 years a makeshift affair, with the guerrillas being pursued from one area to another, suffering heavy casualties, but never being destroyed.

During this 2-year period, duty in the southeast was regarded as relatively safe by the average *Landser* (soldier); not as pleasant, perhaps, as assignment to occupation duty in France, Belgium, or Holland, but infinitely preferable to service in the Soviet Union or North Africa. For its part, the Armed Forces High Command considered its Balkan theater a bulwark against attack from the south and its possession necessary for the security of the forces in the southern part of the Soviet Union. The Reich's primary interest in the area itself, once these security objectives had been achieved, was as a source of strategic raw materials. Its importance increased when the supply of chrome from Turkey was stopped and the Turks began to drift toward the Allied camp.

The German attitude toward the population was one of mistrust. The majority of the inhabitants were Slavs, and *ohne Kultur* (lacking culture). However, as in the other occupied countries, the Germans felt they could reach a *modus vivendi* to achieve their military and political aims; the population could be kept under control by a program of dividing and ruling, well illustrated by the establishment of a Croatian state out of the body of Yugoslavia.

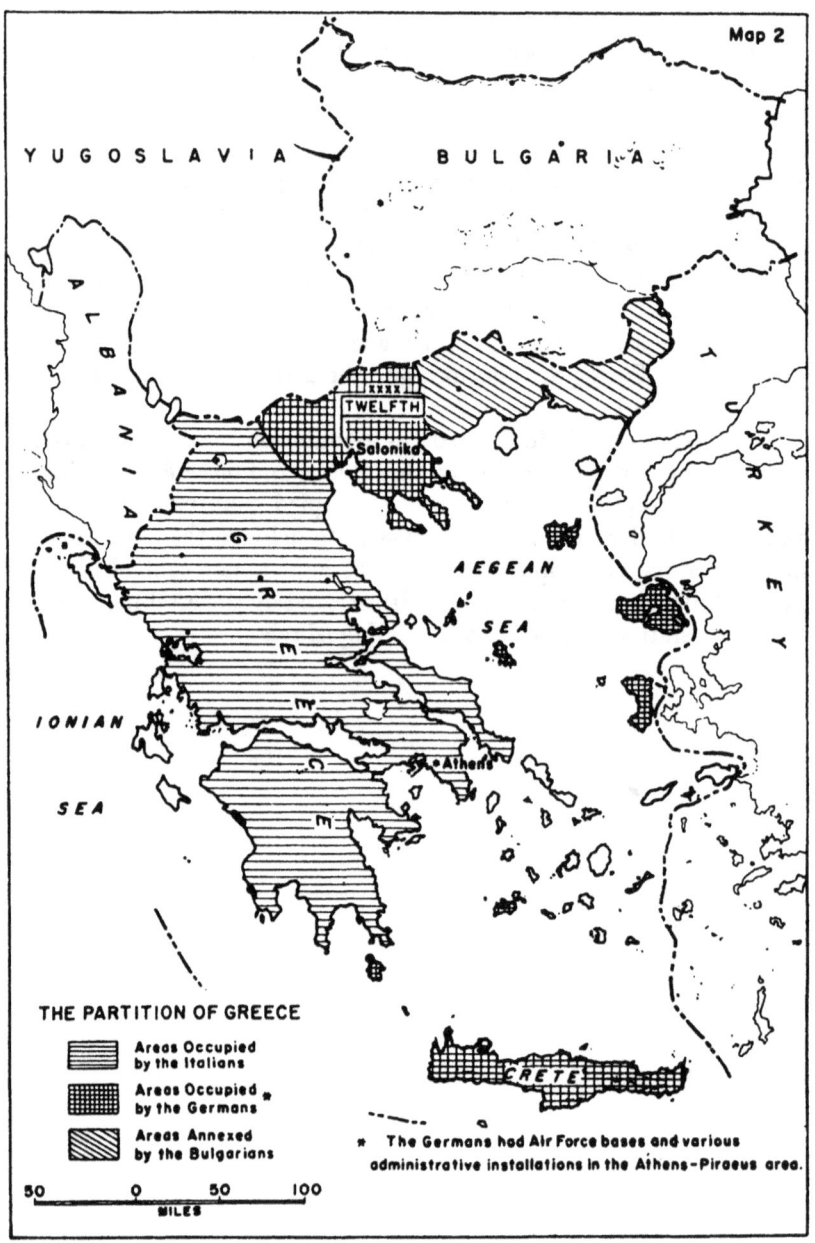

Map 2. *The partition of Greece.*

CHAPTER 4

THE OCCUPATION ZONES AND FORCES

I. Division and Dismemberment

To free German troops for employment in Operation BARBAROSSA and in compliance with commitments to Mussolini, the occupation of the Balkans was to be primarily a responsibility of the Italians. German interests in the area, as defined by Hitler, included only the security of supply routes and communications to German air bases in Greece and Crete, the safeguarding of the copper-producing area in northeastern Serbia, the protection of an open shipping route on the Danube, and retention of the economic privileges granted Germany by the former Yugoslav Government.

In addition to Albania, which they had held since 1939, the Italians assumed control of Greece, with the exception of German-held areas around Salonika and Athens, the island of Crete, and a number of the Aegean Islands. Another exception was western Thrace, which was annexed by the Bulgarians. (Map 2.)

In Yugoslavia, the Italians incorporated western Slovenia, including Ljubljana, into Italy, and annexed Dalmatia and Montenegro. A small portion of southwestern Serbia was detached and added to "Greater Albania." The Italians also dominated the newly proclaimed kingdom of Croatia, which for purposes of security and antiguerrilla operations was divided into German and Italian zones of interest by a line along the axis Visegrad-Sarajevo-Banja Luka-north to the border of the German-annexed portion of Slovenia; the Germans were permitted to send troops into the area east of this line and the Italian troops could operate west of the line. For their part, the Germans incorporated into "Greater Germany" that portion of Slovenia that had once been part of the Austrian province of Carinthia, and occupied Serbia and the Banat. The Bulgarians annexed Yugoslav Macedonia and, in early 1942, occupied southeastern Serbia; the Hungarians annexed the Batchka and Baranya and a small portion of eastern Slovenia. (Map 3.)

II. The Italians

Three Italian armies and a total of 45 divisions had participated in the campaigns against Greece and Yugoslavia. The armies were the Second, Ninth, and Eleventh, all directly under the *Commando*

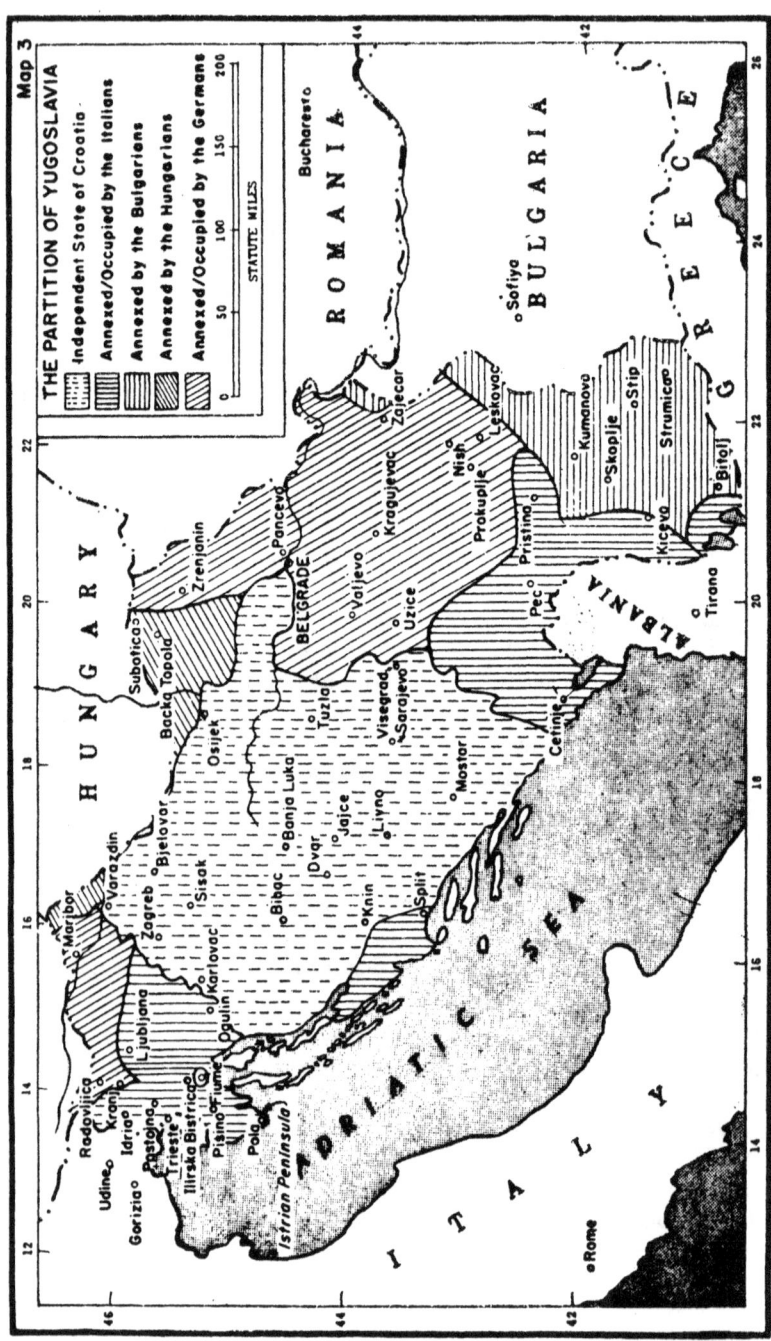

Map 3. The partition of Yugoslavia.

Supremo (Supreme General Staff), under which they remained for the period of the occupation. By early August 1941 the army headquarters had been redesignated as area commands and the total number of divisions redúced to 32. The commander of the Italian Second Army became Armed Forces Commander, Slovenia and Dalmatia, with 8 divisions; the commanding general of the Ninth Army became Armed Forces Commander, Albania and Montenegro, with 12 divisions; the Eleventh Army commander became the Armed Forces Commander, Greece, with 11 divisions. One additional division was stationed in the Dodecanese Islands. A change in this organization was made when the Armed Forces Command, Albania and Montenegro, was divided between the Armed Forces Command, Albania, and the Military Command, Montenegro.

The policy of the Italian occupation authorities was wavering and irresolute, and the Italians accomplished little or nothing toward restoring the economy of the areas under their control. Commanders were slow to react to guerrilla forays, and the common soldier hoped for a state of mutual toleration with the population. This reluctance to act firmly, after their poor showing in the 1940–41 campaigns, earned the Italians the disdain of the Greeks and Yugoslavs and encouraged depredations. Harsh and arbitrary reprisals, when action was undertaken, further increased the resentment of the population toward the Italians. Individual punishment was often inflicted without trial, and on many occasions entire villages were burned to discourage disorders. From disdain, the attitude of the Greeks and Yugoslavs soon changed to one of hatred.

III. The Germans

The German Twelfth Army, which had driven the length of the Balkan Peninsula and conquered Greece, was assigned to the occupation of the German-held areas in the southeast, with headquarters near Athens, whence it moved on 27 October to Salonika. The commander of Twelfth Army, Generalfeldmarschall (Field Marshal) Wilhelm List, also became Armed Forces Commander, Southeast, on 9 June 1941, thereafter functioning in a dual role.[1] As Armed Forces Commander, Southeast, Field Marshal List was the supreme German military authority in the Balkans and was answerable directly to Hitler. His responsibilities in this capacity included the preparation and direction of a coordinated defense against attack, the suppression of internal unrest, and the conduct of relations with the Italian and other Axis military authorities in the area. Marshal List was further charged with the security of German supply routes through the

---
[1] Hereafter the term Armed Forces Commander, Southeast, will be used to refer to the officer holding the title Wehrmachtbefehlshaber Suedost, while the abbreviated title WB Southeast will be used to refer to his headquarters.

Balkans and the military administration of the German-occupied areas. These last were three in number: Serbia proper; the Salonika region and the islands of Lemnos, Mytilene, Khios, and Skyros; and southern Greece, including the cities of Athens and Piraeus, and the islands of Crete, Cythera, and Melos. Serbia was placed under the Military Commander, Serbia, with headquarters at Belgrade; the Salonika area under the Military Commander, Salonika-Aegean, with headquarters at Salonika; and Athens and Piraeus under the Military Commander, Southern Greece, with headquarters at Athens. Since much of the German air effort in the eastern Mediterranean was directed from Athens, the headquarters of the Military Commander, Southern Greece, was staffed largely by the Air Force. The naval and air force headquarters in the Balkans were placed under control of Marshal List for operational purposes, as were the various liaison officers and military missions with the Italians, Bulgarians, Hungarians, and Croats.

At the time hostilities ended in April, Twelfth Army had under its control four corps headquarters and a total of twelve divisions, four of them armored. By 22 June, when Operation BARBAROSSA began, three of the corps headquarters, all the armored divisions, and all but 2 mountain and 1 infantry divisions had been redeployed. This redistribution of forces left Twelfth Army with the XVIII Mountain Corps, with headquarters near Athens, to which were attached the 5th and 6th Mountain Divisions, on Crete and near Athens, respectively; the 164th Infantry Division, in Salonika and on the Aegean Islands; and the 125th Infantry Regiment (Separate), in Salonika.

The gap created by the departed units was filled partially by the recently created LXV Corps Command, an area, rather than a tactical, headquarters stationed in Belgrade. To this headquarters were attached the 704th, 714th, and 717th Infantry Divisions, spread over Serbia proper, and the 718th Infantry Division, stationed in the German zone of interest in Croatia, with headquarters at Banja Luka. (Chart 1.) In contrast to the troops they replaced, more than one-half of the personnel of these divisions, particularly the platoon leaders and noncommissioned officers, were over age for infantry service. The combat experience of most of the company and higher commanders was limited to World War I, and the divisions lacked their full complement of motor vehicles and logistical services. Training had been interrupted by the assignment to occupation duty to the extent one division had only completed battalion exercises.

German strength in the Balkans remained at approximately this level until mid-September 1941, the only change being in mid-August, when the 6th Mountain Division left. The 713th Infantry Division,

CHART No 1- GERMAN GROUND FORCES IN OCCUPIED GREECE AND YUGOSLAVIA
AS OF JULY 1941

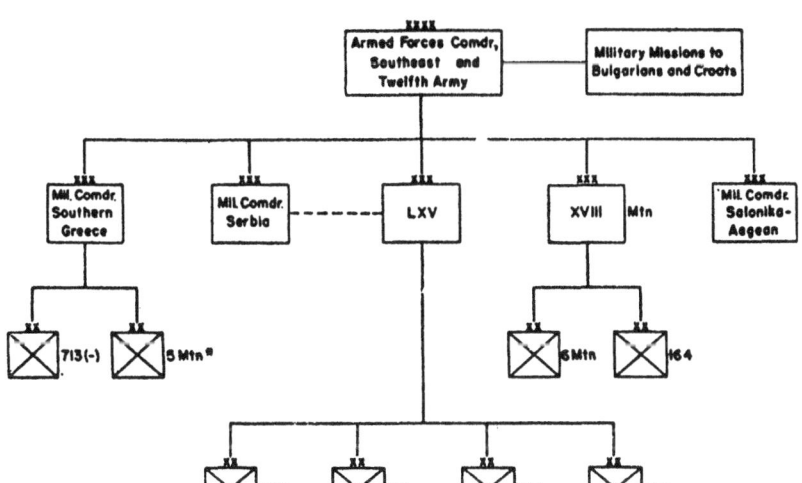

*Normally Attached to XVIII Mountain Corps. Participated in Capture of Crete and Retained Temporarily for Island Defense.

Chart 1.

of the same type as the divisions attached to the LXV Corps Command, moved into the Balkans shortly before the departure of the mountain division.

The military occupation task was made difficult by the presence of various SS and police agencies in the occupied territories. Acting directly under the *Reichsfuehrer SS* and Chief of German Police Himmler, these agencies were the cause of constant irritation to the military commanders. Ostensibly responsible for security, their activities overlapped those of the military, and local commanders were not permitted to control them or to restrict their activities. Various civilian agencies, such as the German Foreign Office, were also represented in Greece and Yugoslavia, further complicating the task of the military commanders.

The policy of the Germans was stern but consistent, compared to that of the Italians. Serbia presented the Germans with a special problem, however, with the traditional Serb hostility to everything Germanic, the rugged independence of the people, and the former position of predominance the Serbs had held in the Yugoslav state

IV. The Bulgarians and Hungarians

To maintain order in their new territories, the Bulgarians dispatched their V Corps, composed of three divisions, to Yugoslav

Macedonia, and their I Corps to Thrace. A subsequent reassignment of units, with the movement of Bulgarian troops into the German zone in Yugoslavia, brought the I Corps to southeastern Serbia and a provisional "Aegean Corps" to Thrace. Later in the war, the Aegean Corps was relieved by the II Corps. A number of incidents involving the native population in Macedonia caused the Bulgarians to turn from a benevolent to a harsh policy of pacification. In Greece, where they felt they were recovering territory lost to the Greeks in the Second Balkan War of 1913, the policy of the Bulgarians was arbitrary and severe from the outset of the occupation.

The Hungarians occupied several small areas of Yugoslavia to the west and south of Hungary, and immediately incorporated them into their national state. Inhabited by large Hungarian minorities, these territories had formed part of the Austro-Hungarian Empire until 1918, hence the Hungarian attitude toward the population was far more lenient than that of the other occupation forces in their respective zones.

V. The Puppet Governments

Puppet regimes were installed to lighten the administrative burden of the occupied areas and exploit the differences between the various Greek and Yugoslav national and political factions. Native police, security forces, and national armies were also organized to reduce the number of occupation troops required to keep order and protect the various new governments.

The collaborationist regime in Greece was organized under the premiership of General Tsolakoglou, who had surrendered the Army of Epirus to the Germans on 20 April 1941. Although this government formed police and security units and actively assisted the German and Italian occupiers, it did not organize armed forces on a national scale.

In Croatia a kingdom was organized under the nominal rule of the absentee Italian Duke of Spoleto, with actual authority vested in Ante Pavelitch, the *Poglavnik* (Prime Minister), who began his administration with a ruthless persecution of the Serbian minority within the borders of the new Croatian state.

Pavelitch, living in exile under Italian sponsorship, had been indirectly involved in the assassination of King Alexander of Yugoslavia at Marseilles in 1934. Arriving in Croatia in the wake of the Germans in 1941 with fewer than a hundred of his *Ustascha*, a politico-military group similar to the Italian Blackshirts, Pavelitch quickly organized a political army of 15 battalions, and a Ustascha Guard of 1 infantry regiment and a cavalry squadron. Under the aegis of the Italian authorities, he also began the conscription of a national military force, which did not progress beyond eight mountain and light infantry brigades and a railroad security brigade until late in the war, when these brigades were joined with the expanded Ustascha forces to form divisions. Croatian-German "Legion" units, such as the 369th, 373d, and 392d Infantry Divisions; two SS divisions, the 13th and 23d Mountain; and additional mountain brigades and separate battalions were recruited in Croatia by the Germans draining off much of the manpower that might have gone to the Croatian forces. More potential Croatian troops were siphoned off in labor drafts or by the police, or fled to join one or another of the guerrilla groups.

A Petain-like figure was found in Serbia in the person of General Neditch, a former chief of staff of the Royal Yugoslav Army. Within Serbia, in addition to the civil police, several militarized security forces were formed to keep order and lighten the German occupation task. The first of these was the Border Guard, 5,600 strong, including a German cadre of 600; the primary mission of this force was to control traffic across the Serbian frontier. In addition, to support the city and rural police should the need arise, the State Guard was organized, comprising five battalions with an authorized total strength of 3,560 men.

The Serbian Volunteer Battalions, later amalgamated into the Serbian Volunteer Corps, most closely approximated a national military force. Four and later five in number, these battalions, under the command of General Ljotitch, were scattered about the German-occupied area of Serbia. Their approximate total strength was 2,000.

Another force formed in 1941 within Serbia but not responsible to the Neditch Government was the Russian Guard Corps, under command of General Steifon. It had three regiments and a total strength of 4,000. Incorporated into the Wehrmacht, the corps was composed largely of anti-Soviet émigrés who had served in the armies of the Czar; many of the personnel were incapable of extended field service, and the Germans generally restricted them to such security duties as the protection of the vital Belgrade-Nish railroad line.

CHAPTER 5

THE EARLY MOVEMENT AND AXIS COUNTERMEASURES

The political allegiances of the resistance movement had little influence on the military operations conducted by the occupying powers. Rather, everyone fighting against the occupation forces was considered a threat to their hold on the Balkans. True, the methods used and the ultimate objectives differed from one group to the other. However, as far as the Italians, Germans, and Bulgarians were concerned, all in arms against them were enemies, whether they wore the royal crest of a sovereign in exile, the hammer and sickle, or no insignia whatever.

I. Yugoslavia

Armed opposition on a significant scale received its start in Yugoslavia. However, any consideration of this movement would be incomplete without distinguishing between the Pan-Serb, monarchical group of the former Col. Draja Mihailovitch and the communist-led effort of Josip Broz, or Tito. It was the former that first came to the attention of the Allied world, at the time German domination of the Continent was almost complete and Soviet forces were retreating from western Russia.

Mihailovitch called his irregulars "Chetniks," from the title of a Serb nationalist organization that had resisted the Turks, fought well in World War I, and since existed as a reserve force to be called up when needed. Costa Pecanatch, the aging World War I leader, went over to the Neditch government at the outset of the occupation, leaving Mihailovitch with those remnants willing to resist the occupation forces and collaborationists. The Mihailovitch movement quickly gained momentum during the early summer of 1941, and liaison was established with the government-in-exile of King Peter. A short time later Mihailovitch was first named commander of the resistance forces within Yugoslavia, and then minister of defense of the royal government-in-exile.

Chetnik policy called for the organization of strong underground forces in Serbia for the day when they might rise in conjunction with Allied landings on the Balkan Peninsula. Mihailovitch, himself, had been appalled by the execution of some 35,000 Serb hostages for Chetnik activities in World War I, and was determined to avoid repetition of any such reprisals for a premature rising of the forces under his command. Thus, Chetnik operations were generally restricted to small-scale actions and sabotage.

It was the communist irregulars who adopted the name of Partisan and made it synonymous with guerrilla. Under Tito, born Josip Broz in Croatia, converted to communism while a prisoner of war of the Russians at the time of the Red Revolution, and Secretary General of the Communist Party of Yugoslavia since 1937, the Partisan movement received its start in Belgrade immediately after the surrender to the Germans. In August 1941 Tito moved his headquarters into the field and took over command of the growing Partisan forces. The antiroyalist policy of the Partisans and anticommunist attitude of the Chetniks soon led to a fratricidal conflict between the two, a cleavage the Germans were quick to turn to their own advantage. Whereas the Chetniks comprised mostly local units to be called up as needed, the Partisans had a great number of large and active mobile units capable of moving about the country and not tied down to any particular locality. As a consequence, the Partisans were not as hesitant as the Chetniks to engage in operations for which the occupying forces would exact severe reprisals, a development that incurred further the enmity of the Chetniks. A conflict within a conflict soon developed, with one Yugoslav force attacking the other while that force was already engaged against occupation troops.

In some cases the Partisans were given credit for Chetnik attacks against the occupation forces and their auxiliaries; on the other hand, the Chetniks were credited with successful Partisan forays. To complicate matters further, there were also guerrilla bands operating under no other authority than their own. Thus, German references to Partisans did not necessarily mean the forces of Tito, but rather the Yugoslav resistance forces in general, regardless of political sympathies. As well as the European Axis came to know them, it could not always distinguish one group from the other, and came to use the word Partisan in its broadest sense.

The most important guerrilla operation in 1941 took place against the Italians in Montenegro. Ruggedly independent, the Montenegrins on 13 July swarmed down in well-coordinated attacks on the Italian garrisons scattered throughout their mountain state. Taken by surprise, the occupation forces were destroyed or thrown back on their major garrison towns and communications centers. Returning with strong ground, naval, and air forces, the Italians required almost a year to put down the rising, and managed to accomplish it only by enlisting the aid of the Chetniks. Stipulations in the agreement with local Chetnik leaders required the Italians to restrict themselves to the garrison towns and main communication and transportation lines.

In turn, the Chetniks maintained control over the countryside and kept it free of Partisans, drawing on Italian stocks for arms and ammunition.

This general rising cost the Montenegrins dearly—15,000 dead and wounded and an additional 10,000 of the sparse mountain population shipped off to forced labor. The arrangement with the Chetniks also set the pattern for the Italian occupation—troops seldom moved out of the garrison towns, and then only along the main roads and in strength, accompanied by armored vehicles and often under air cover.

One other major countermeasure by the Italian occupation forces against the irregulars was undertaken in July of 1942 when Generale di Corpo D'Armata (Lieutenant General) Mario Robotti launched a drive against the Partisans in Slovenia. Committing 7 army divisions, 2 Blackshirt battalions, and Slovene auxiliaries, General Robotti managed to surround the enemy. Several thousand casualties were inflicted on the Partisans, and the survivors were routed. The Partisan movement in Slovenia in this operation suffered a setback from which it did not recover for months.

Guerrilla activities against the Germans in Yugoslavia commenced shortly after the cessation of formal hostilities. However, in the beginning, open resistance to the German forces was on a smaller scale than in the Italian-occupied areas, and the guerrillas conducted themselves more cautiously. With the departure, by late June 1941, of the bulk of the combat troops for Operation BARBAROSSA, the WB Southeast reported an increasing number of sabotage incidents. Road and railroad bridges were blown; telephone and telegraph lines were cut; trains derailed; German military vehicles, traveling either alone or in convoy, fired on or destroyed; and isolated detachments guarding industrial and military installations attacked. During July and August there were also daily attacks on Serbian police posts to obtain weapons and on villages to obtain food. Standing crops were burned, banks robbed, and a general state of uncertainty and unrest created.

A number of small-scale operations by the 704th, 714th, 717th, and 718th Infantry Divisions, dispersed over Serbia and the German zone of interest in Croatia, resulted in a large number of casualties and arrests, but accomplished little in effectively curbing the guerrilla movement. Nor did the shooting of hostages or burning of homes of suspects and whole communities suspected of sheltering the guerrillas achieve the desired results. By 5 September the WB Southeast realized that the situation could not be mastered with the forces at hand and ordered the 125th Infantry Regiment (Separate) from the Salonika area to Belgrade.

It was now obvious that a strong, well-organized, and adequately armed revolt was underway in northwestern Serbia, and that the remainder of German-occupied Serbia was seriously threatened The spreading disorders were also affecting the supply of vital raw materials, to the extent that in the third quarter of 1941 the destruction of installations in the Bor mining area (northeast of Nish) caused a production loss of nearly a month's requirement of copper for the German war industries. In view of this increasingly critical situation, the Armed Forces Commander, Southeast, was forced to concentrate his meager and scattered forces for the defense of those cities, industrial installations, and transportation lines considered most vital to the German occupation. Further, he requested that the Armed Forces High Command have established a unified command for operations in Serbia under the commander of the XVIII Mountain Corps, General der Gebirgstruppen (Lieutenant General) Franz Boehme. Marshal List further recommended that General Boehme be assigned a combat infantry division and armored support, to supplement the divisions immediately available.

In response to this request, on 16 September Hitler issued a directive that charged Marshal List with suppressing the revolt in the southeast. To accomplish this, he was to place General Boehme in complete charge of operations in Serbia and the adjacent areas in which the irregulars had established themselves. General Boehme was to have command of all troops in the area and of any others that might be moved in; all military and civil authorities were required to carry out General Boehme's orders insofar as they pertained to his mission. The Army High Command was ordered to reinforce the troops in Serbia by one infantry division, armored trains, captured tanks, and further security forces; other captured tanks and security troops were to be sent to Croatia. Another infantry division from the Eastern Front was to be transferred to Serbia when it became available. The Hungarian, Romanian, and Bulgarian forces could be called upon to assist in the operations with the permission of the Armed Forces High Command; the use of Croatian forces available in the German zone of interest adjacent to the Serbian border was approved. The Italians had been informed of the contemplated operations and had been asked to cooperate. In addition, the German Foreign Office was simultaneously to carry out a political offensive in cooperation with the puppet and allied governments against communist centers in the Balkan countries.

Implementation of this directive followed swiftly. Three days later General Boehme moved with his headquarters from Salonika and assumed command in Belgrade, and less than one week following this the 342d Infantry Division arrived from Germany.

A series of vigorous offensive operations begun by General Boehme succeeded in quelling the open revolt in western Serbia and inflicting over 2,000 casualties on the guerrillas by mid-December. For these operations, General Boehme committed the 342d Infantry Division; the 125th Infantry Regiment (Separate); the 113th Infantry Division, which had arrived from Germany late in November; and the 704th and 714th Infantry Divisions. The guerrillas, however, were not annihilated; large numbers fled into the more mountainous regions and into Croatia, where a new center of open revolt was soon formed.

As of 25 October, Marshal List had been forced to relinquish his duties because of illness, and General der Pioniere (Lieutenant General) Walter Kuntze was appointed acting Armed Forces Commander, Southeast. In early December orders were received to move the XVIII Mountain Corps, the only tactical corps headquarters in the southeast, to Germany. General Boehme's command functions in Serbia were transferred to the commander of the LXV Corps Command, General der Artillerie (Lieutenant General) Paul Bader.

This loss was shortly followed by another, when the serious situation in Russia made necessary the transfer of both the 342d and 113th Infantry Divisions by the end of January 1942. This reduction of forces prompted the German Armed Forces High Command to request the Bulgarians to move troops into southeastern Serbia. The Bulgarians assented and immediately shifted their I Corps from Thrace. Since it was occupying that part of Serbia allocated as an occupation zone of the Germans, the Bulgarian I Corps later came under the operational control of the German Military Commander, Serbia.

The Bulgarian command in Yugoslavia had a pacification problem similar to that of the Germans. Consequently, the Bulgarians undertook a number of antiguerrilla operations on their own initiative, informing the Germans through liaison officers of the results of their efforts. In general, these were so savage as to quell the growth of any resistance movement of significance until late the following year.

Croatia, with its own armed forces, had little success in putting down the spreading Partisan movement within its borders during late 1941. By the end of the year, additional German troops had crossed the borders of the new state into the German zone of interest in order to cooperate with the Ustascha and Croat national forces in hunting down the Partisans in the southeastern part of the country. Resistance to the Croat troops was intensified by their persecution of the Serbian minority. The Italian Second Army was of little help in restoring order; Italian units in the area assisting the Germans and Croats showed more interest in occupying important transportation and communication centers than in clearing Croatia of the guerrillas.

With Serbia quiet and the guerrilla forces active in their zone of interest in Croatia, the Germans planned a large-scale operation designed to annihilate the guerrillas in place or drive them into strong Italian blocking forces to be brought up to the Italian side of the demarcation line. Planned for mid-January 1942, the operation would have the advantage of cold weather, inconvenient for the Germans but disastrous for the guerrillas, who lacked proper clothing and equipment for operations in the snow. Also, the 342d Infantry Division would be available, just prior to its departure for Russia.

Well planned and typical of antiguerrilla measures of the period, the operation was conducted from 15 to 26 January, with the 342d and 718th Infantry Divisions, as well as Croatian national forces, participating. The guerrillas were estimated at 4,000, concentrated about Sarajevo and Visegrad and the area to the north. Meeting strong resistance, the Germans suffered a total of 25 dead, 131 wounded, and almost 300 cases of frostbite, against 521 guerrilla dead and 1,331 captured. Booty included 855 rifles, 22 machine guns, 4 field pieces, 600 head of livestock, and 33 draft animals. A tactical success, the operation failed to achieve its purpose when the Italian forces against which the guerrillas were to be driven did not arrive in time to prevent the escape of large numbers of the guerrillas into the Italian zone of interest in Croatia.

Reports from German commanders who had participated indicated that the Croatian troops could perform satisfactorily only when integrated with German units, and that the Croat officers and noncommissioned officers lacked training and tactical ability. The escape of entire guerrilla units also made obvious the need for a combined command, with authority over all German, Italian, Croatian, and other forces participating. On one occasion, during the operation, Italian airmen bombed a German-held village, whereupon the Germans requested Italian air support be withdrawn. Another mistake was the assignment of Ustascha troops to areas populated mainly by Serbs. Finally, the understrength German divisions (two regiments of infantry rather than the normal three) in the "700 series" in the southeast lacked personnel and staying power for sustained operations against strong guerrilla forces.

Sharp fighting at Valjevo in February caused the Germans almost 500 casualties, as against over 3,500 guerrillas killed in action or shot in reprisal. Lacking troops, it was obvious that General Kuntze would require the assistance of the Italians and Croatians if his meager forces in Croatia were to quell the disorders in the German zone of interest.

A trip to Hitler's headquarters and to Italy was instrumental in securing approval for a combined German-Italian-Croatian operation to clear east Bosnia. General Bader, now commanding all German forces and the administrative area in Serbia, was named task force commander, under operational control of the Italian Second Army for the period of the operation.² His force was to consist of three Italian divisions, the German 718th Infantry Division, German units from Serbia, and Croatian national troops. Extending from 20 April to 3 May, the operation was considered a success from the German standpoint, with 168 enemy dead, 1,309 prisoners taken, and stocks of weapons, ammunition, and equipment captured. However, large numbers of guerrillas managed to escape through the Italian units assigned to block their flight and to make their way into the Italian zone of interest in Croatia. Task Force Bader was disbanded upon conclusion of the operation, and its commander returned to Serbia.

Another operation, to clear west Bosnia, was scheduled for June. The task force commander, Generalmajor (Brigadier General) Friedrich Stahl, commanding the 714th Infantry Division, organized his combat elements around three German infantry battalions with artillery support and two Croatian mountain brigades. No exact figures on casualties were given, but the cost to the guerrillas was high and the undertaking was regarded as a success by the Germans. The lack of experience and tactical ability on the part of the Croat troops were made glaringly obvious during the operation, when the two mountain brigades broke in disorder and German troops had to strengthen them.

Following the conclusion of the operation in west Bosnia, the divisions in Serbia and Croatia were redisposed. While the 718th Infantry Division remained in east Bosnia, the 714th Infantry Division was assigned to west Bosnia. The 704th Infantry Division remained in eastern Serbia, and the 717th Infantry Division was shifted from southwestern to northwestern Serbia. In turn, the 7th SS Mountain Division (Prinz Eugen), recently formed with ethnic German personnel from Yugoslavia and Romania, was assigned the area evacuated by the 717th Division.

The modest successes of the recent German operations in Bosnia were offset at this time by the withdrawal of the Italian garrisons disposed along the Italian side of the German-Italian demarcation line. The military vacuum created in the area by this withdrawal was immediately used to advantage by the guerrillas, who now had no occupation force with which to contend. The withdrawal was in accordance with an earlier Italian decision to reduce their Second Army garrisons and relinquish control of the interior of Croatia to Croat national forces. To this end, the Italian command had divided its zone of interest into three areas, numbered from one to three, and roughly parallel to the demarcation line and the coast. The third zone, adjoining the German area of interest, was abandoned first, despite German protests that guerrilla activities would increase.

---

² On 1 March the headquarters of the LXV Corps Command and the Military Commander, Serbia were merged.

A German recapitulation of casualties sustained by the Yugoslav guerrillas from the beginning of the occupation to July 1942 estimated the total at 45,000 dead, with thousands more sent off to forced labor in Germany and occupied areas as far away as Norway, or detained in internment camps. In addition to the arrestees shipped out of the country, the Germans added a large number of former Yugoslav officers as a security measure, whether or not any involvement with the guerrillas could be proved against them.

The German forces in Croatia and Serbia carried on a series of small-scale operations throughout the remainder of the year without achieving any marked success in eliminating the guerrilla movement. There was an increase in troop strength when the 187th Reserve Division arrived in Croatia by December. (Chart 2.) In October, a new

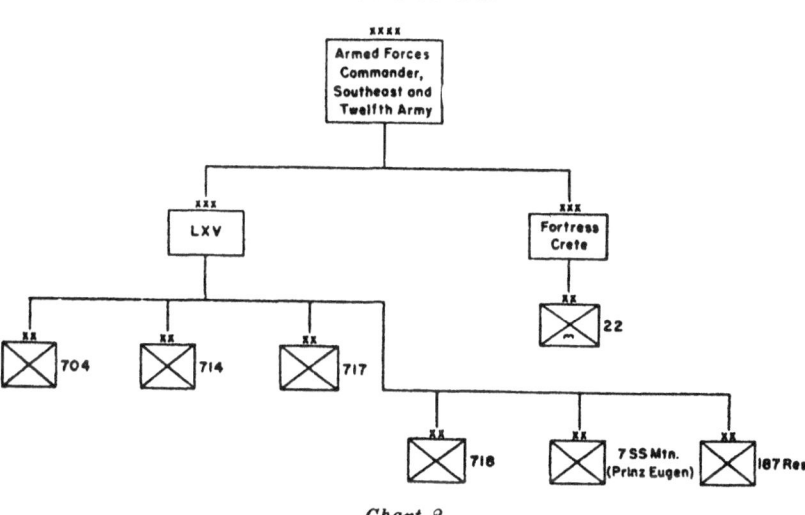

Chart 2.

headquarters, that of Commander of German Troops in Croatia, under Generalleutnant (Major General) Rudolf Lueters, was created; however, this headquarters did not become operational until shortly after the end of the year.

II. Greece

The Greek resistance movement, like the Yugoslav, was divided along political lines between the groups adhering to the royal government-in-exile and those led or strongly influenced by communists. In Greece the former were led by a Colonel Zervas, a retired officer of the Greek Regular Army; the latter, by a Colonel Sarafis, dismissed from the Regular Army for political activities in January 1935. The

Zervas organization, known as EDES (Greek Democratic National League), was restricted to the mountains of Epirus in northwestern Greece; ELAS (Greek People's Liberation Army) operated in the rest of the country. While EDES maintained contact with the Greek Government-in-Exile, ELAS functioned under EAM (National Liberation Front), a coalition of left-wing parties with a hard core of Communists. Another guerrilla group, socialist in nature and associated loosely with ELAS, was known as EKKA (National and Social Liberation); it was led by a Colonel Psarros and operated in central Greece.

Unlike those in Yugoslavia, the Greek guerrillas undertook no operations of importance in 1941. For their part, the Germans were more concerned with fortifying Crete, pursuing their air effort in the eastern Mediterranean from Greek bases, and getting all combat forces that could be spared to the more active theaters of war. In late October the 5th Mountain Division was moved from Crete to Germany, being replaced by the weak 164th and 713th Infantry Divisions from the Athens and Salonika areas; these two divisions were then disbanded to form Fortress Division, Crete. The garrison on Crete received further reinforcement in the 125th Infantry Regiment (Separate), moved down from Serbia, where it had proved itself in heavy antiguerrilla fighting.

An example of guerrilla operations in Greece in 1942 is provided by an attack of the Zervas group on an Italian supply column on the Yannina–Arta road during the summer. (Map 4.) This completely successful attack, in which approximately one hundred guerrillas annihilated a heavily armed force of sixty men and captured or destroyed a large stock of ammunition and gasoline, was carefully prepared and vigorously executed. The attack was made under difficult conditions, in that Italian forces were in control of the area and had held it for more than a year, allowing them ample opportunity to recruit informants, know the population well enough to detect new arrivals, and reconnoiter the terrain. In addition, the Italians were amply supplied with signal equipment, automatic weapons, and armored vehicles, while the guerrillas had not yet captured any appreciable number of arms or received any substantial supplies from the Allies. Except for a few machineguns and mines, the only weapons of the attackers were rifles and dynamite.

After several weeks of studying Italian dispositions and movements in the area, the guerrillas decided that an attack on the heavily loaded supply column regularly carrying gasoline and ammunition from Yannina to Arta offered the best prospect of success. Accordingly, the guerrilla command chose a defile along the road, out of sight of any inhabited locality, where rocky ledges on either side offered cover to ambushers. Mines could be used to stop the lead vehicle, while a bridge to the rear could be blown to block the column's withdrawal.

On the day of the attack, the guerrillas occupied their hiding places before daylight and waited throughout the day. Telephone and telegraph poles along the road had been cut almost through, so that they could be pulled down with little effort just prior to the action, effectively eliminating any wire communication between the garrisons at Arta and Yannina. Large boulders had been rolled into position on the higher ledges and so placed as to require only a slight pressure to send them tumbling down onto the column halted below. The few machineguns were sited to allow enfilading fire the length of the column, while the gun crews had the protection of the stone ledges against flat trajectory fire from below.

The Italian column appeared at 1600 and was halted exactly as planned when the lead vehicle, a tank, was disabled by mines. The last vehicle, also a tank, was trapped when the bridge behind it was blown a minute later. The column commander became a casualty almost immediately, and the alarmed troops added to the confusion by firing their automatic weapons blindly at the ledges above. The only organized resistance, which caused a number of casualties to the attackers, came from the crew of the tank at the tail of the column; this vehicle was soon put out of action by a dynamite charge. After raking the column repeatedly with heavy fire, the guerrillas swarmed down onto the roadway and slaughtered the few dazed Italians remaining; no prisoners were taken. The supplies carried by the column were quickly loaded onto pack animals brought up for the purpose, while roadblocks secured the attackers against surprise by relief columns from Arta or Yannina.

As planned by the attackers, approaching darkness made pursuit impossible. A motorcycle platoon sent out from Arta to investigate the disruption of wire communications was stopped by fire at the roadblock south of the site of the ambush and no further relief was attempted until morning, by which time the guerrillas were safely away.

Although the supply column had been heavily armed, the Italian commander had made a mistake that was often to cost the occupation forces heavily—he had followed a fixed pattern in moving critical supplies along the same route at regular intervals, making it possible for the guerrillas to determine the schedule, the strength of the escort, and observe the practice of having the only armored vehicles at the head and tail. Such successful attacks emboldened the resistance forces and inclined recruits to join their ranks or to assist them in various other ways, such as reporting troop movements.

During July and August, Fortress Division Crete was sent to Africa, and redesignated the 164th Light Africa Division. In its place, the

22d Airborne Division was moved in from Russia and assigned to garrison the island fortress.

On 8 August, the acting Armed Forces Commander, Southeast, General Kuntze, was relieved by Generaloberst (General) Alexander Loehr. General Loehr, a Luftwaffe officer, had been in command of the Fourth Air Force in Russia before receiving his new appointment as commander in the Balkans; he had also commanded the task force which captured Crete in May 1941.

Guerrilla operations in Greece were not restricted to ambushes. Sabotage, particularly along the vital Athens–Salonika rail line, also played an important part in hampering the supply of the occupation forces and tying down units to perform security duties. The most significant sabotage operation was executed on 25 November, when a small guerrilla force overpowered Italian guards and blew up the Gorgopotamos Bridge, some hundred miles north of Athens. This successful operation not only halted the flow of supplies until repairs could be effected, but led to severe criticism of the Italians by the Germans and made it necessary for the Germans to take over the security of a long stretch of this rail line in Italian-occupied territory, a strain on the already insufficient German forces and a rebuff to Italian pride.

Additional troops were moved into the Greek area in December, as a result of the Allied landings in Africa one month earlier. The threat presented by United States and British forces to his position in the eastern Mediterranean prompted Hitler shortly afterward to direct immediate reinforcements to be sent to General Loehr. Accordingly, the 11th Luftwaffe Field Division moved into Attica, north of Athens,[3] Though the original purpose in sending the 11th Field Division to Greece had been to replace the 22d Airborne Division, the worsening strategic situation required the retention of both divisions. As a result, the 11th Field Division took over responsibility for a considerable area of Attica and the 22d Division remained as a mobile and potent striking force to counter possible Allied landings on Crete.

By the end of 1942, the Greek resistance forces were still in the process of formation, having no centralized command. While Chetniks and Partisans in Yugoslavia had already established higher headquarters to direct operations, and were receiving quantities of supplies from the British forces in the Middle East, the Greek resistance units were recruiting personnel and leaders of such stature as to command the respect and win the support of the population.

---

[3] Luftwaffe field divisions were composed of Air Force personnel. They were organized as Army divisions and used in an infantry role.

CHAPTER 6

ORGANIZATION OF GUERRILLA UNITS

1. Unit and Command Structure

Most of the early guerrilla groups in Greece and Yugoslavia were organized on a regional basis, taking as a unit designation the name of their leader or of the area, or of such geographical features as forests or mountains. In time, such leaders as Zervas, Sarafis, Mihailovitch, and Tito arose, and the various groups divided along political lines. As they expanded, it became necessary to form military units.

In Greece the units were organized and designated along the lines of the regular forces of the prewar period, with companies, battalions, regiments, and divisions. In Yugoslavia the *odreds* (groups) became brigades, above which higher headquarters were formed to exercise control. Since the forces in both countries were still on a militia basis, the Greek and Yugoslav commands also found it expedient to form mobile units, which would not be tied down to any particular region and could be sent where needed. Captured arms, as well as materiel supplied by the Allies, soon permitted the mobile units to take on the semblance of regular troops, with automatic weapons, mortars, antitank guns, and even light field pieces to support their riflemen. The military designations of brigade, division, and corps, however, were no indication of actual strength. For example, ELAS at one time had 10 organizations carried as divisions, but a total strength of only 30,000; the brigades of Tito's Partisans frequently had only a few hundred men.

In the Partisan force, the chain of command went through brigade, division, corps, and area headquarters, and then to Tito's staff, which had a status comparable to that of an army. Tito himself professed to be the commander of the armed forces of the independent state of Yugoslavia.

The Chetnik organization was based on a "brigade" of two combat companies and a replacement company. Three to eight brigades formed a corps, subordinate to an area headquarters responsible to Mihailovitch, at approximately army level. As Yugoslav Minister of Defense, Mihailovitch was a member of the Yugoslav Government-in-Exile and responsible to the Prime Minister and King Peter.

Authority in ELAS extended from company through division, also an area command, to ELAS headquarters, which was comparable to a corps with ten divisions. When ELAS reached this point in its development, intermediate headquarters—so-called groups of divisions—were formed, and ELAS headquarters assumed army status. The Central Committee of EAM, in turn, exercised executive direction over ELAS headquarters.

The EDES group by the end of 1942 comprised only a battalion and a number of smaller units. EDES headquarters itself was subordinated to the British Middle East forces and the Greek Government-in-Exile.

A number of attempts were made, chiefly by the Allies, to combine the efforts of the rival Greek and Yugoslav guerrilla armies. Although a combined Greek headquarters was actually formed and functioned for a time, opposing political aspirations soon brought ELAS and EDES into open conflict with one another again. In Yugoslavia, attempts to unite the Chetnik and Partisan movements progressed no farther than a brief conference between Tito and Mihailovitch at the town of Uzice in 1941.

II. Communications and Supply

Closely connected with the command structure was the problem of signal communications. For forces like the Greek and Yugoslav guerrilla units, fighting for survival in enemy-occupied territory, adequate communications were vital. Since the occupation troops were in possession of the telegraph stations, telephone exchanges, and such radio transmitters as existed in the two countries, the resistance leaders were forced to rely on two other media of communication, courier and radio. Where the former sufficed for short-range work and the delivery of funds and some messages, it could hardly be used for frequent communication between widely separated units and with Allied headquarters across the Mediterranean and Adriatic Seas. Therefore, despite difficulties in transmission and reception in mountain areas, the various guerrilla leaders came to make increasing use of the air waves. For security reasons they did much of their own cryptographic work, until Allied liaison teams with trained personnel were assigned to them. However, a considerable volume of transmission between units was still carried on in the clear by poorly trained native operators, and the Germans were not slow to seize upon the opportunity to gain information. For example, within 60 days of setting up its monitoring devices, one German intercept platoon was able to compile the complete order of battle of the Chetnik forces, including identification and strength of major units, names of commanders, and locations of headquarters.

As the irregular forces grew in size, the problem of feeding increased apace. Since Greece was a food-importing country even in peacetime, the situation in that country was particularly acute. In Yugoslavia, which normally had a surplus and exported large quantities of grain, the matter of rations was critical only in certain unproductive areas such as the mountains of Bosnia, or in localities where the occupation forces had seized and removed large stocks of food.

A distinction must also be made between the static and mobile guerrilla units; the former lived as peasants or tradesmen when not engaged in operations and could support themselves, while the latter had to remain in hiding and could seldom provide their own sustenance. The mobile units then began the practice of requisitioning food in rural areas, since sufficient rations could not be acquired from captured stores and the Allied airlift brought in mostly weapons, ammunition, explosives, and other combat equipment. In the early period, villages in each group's area were assessed specified quantities of produce, which were usually picked up at night. On occasion the guerrilla groups clashed with one another when one group encroached upon another's territory to procure food supplies; sometimes the peasants themselves resisted requisitioning.

As old Greek and Yugoslav uniforms wore out, the guerrillas turned to the occupation forces and civilian population for replacements. In time, a large number of the irregulars were clad in pieces of German and Italian uniforms or cast-off civilian clothing. Later, when supplies in bulk were received from the Allies, many of the guerrillas were issued one-piece khaki uniforms, on which they wore as insignia the royal arms or the hammer and sickle, with or without designation of rank.

The first Allied liaison officers had been assigned to Yugoslav resistance units by late 1941 and to the Greeks in the course of 1942. As these units cleared larger areas of occupation forces, it soon became possible to bring in increasing quantities of materiel and supplies by air. Requests for specific equipment and stores were made by guerrilla commanders to the liaison officers, and transmitted to the British forces in the Middle East and later to Allied Forces Headquarters in Italy. Supplies were also moved in by submarine and small boat along unguarded stretches of the coast.

III. Training and Tactics

The training of the guerrillas centered about the use of rifles and light automatic weapons, the laying of mines, and the preparation of demolitions. Former members of the Greek and Yugoslav forces usually received about 2 weeks of instruction. However, as casualties mounted and the guerrilla forces grew in size, many youths with no previous military experience were enlisted and given from 4 to 6 weeks of basic training. The intensity of training depended to a large extent on the ability of the local commander and the need for the troops in operations.

Shortage of ammunition often required that firing be held to the minimum during training. In addition to work with his individual weapon, the guerrilla also learned to lay mines, plant demolition charges, and execute ambushes. Night marches and stealth in movement were stressed, and the guerrillas were instructed never to abandon their dead or wounded to the enemy. Security was also given proper emphasis, and in communist units political indoctrination filled a large part of the training schedule.

Discipline was strict, with lesser crimes punished by public admonition, loss of rank, relief from command, or prohibition from bearing arms for a specified period of time. Serious offenses, such as treason and cowardice, were punished by death, the execution being carried out by the offender's immediate superior.

Attacks were carefully planned, taking full advantage of any weakness or carelessness of the occupation forces. The tactic most commonly practiced was the ambush, so timed that the attackers would be well away before the arrival of any relief: mobile units would retire to prearranged hiding places, and the militiamen would return to their homes and regular occupations.

Laying mines and planting demolitions by night were other operations favored by the guerrillas. Designed to cripple transportation and communications and cause casualties, these tactics also tied down engineer personnel who might have been put to other tasks or made available for assignment to active fronts.

Sniping at individual soldiers and small parties also was common practice, as was the cutting of telephone lines and the mining of poles that had to be climbed before repairs could be effected. In the latter case, the lineman working in his exposed position on the pole could be shot if the mine were not effective.

Finally, there was an almost universal disregard on the part of the guerrilla forces, particularly the communists, for the accepted customs and usages of war. Hospitals, ambulance convoys, and hospital trains, lacking any protection but the small arms carried by officers and enlisted orderlies, were easy targets to attack and particularly inviting, since the guerrillas suffered from a chronic shortage of medical supplies. The sick and wounded would be slain in their beds, the medical stores looted, and on occasion captured doctors and other medical personnel would be carried along and forced to care for sick and wounded guerrillas. The shortage of clothing and the necessity of obtaining uniforms for purposes of disguise soon made the stripping of all corpses a common practice, and extremists among the irregulars would mutilate both living and dead in exacting personal vengeance. These acts of terrorism incurred savage retaliation by the Germans and their allies, and increased the fury of the struggle.

PART THREE

THE GUERRILLA MOVEMENT IN GREECE, YUGOSLAVIA, AND ALBANIA (1943-44)

The German prospect of victory had begun to fade by the beginning of 1943. Stalingrad would cost the Germans 22 divisions and 300,000 men of the Sixth Army by February, and Axis forces in North Africa would be forced to surrender to the Allies in May. The growing losses on all fronts could no longer be replaced in full, and Fortress Europe was threatened by invasion from the south. In their zones of Greece and Yugoslavia, the Germans were plagued by attacks on small outposts and transportation lines, sapping their strength, tying down units and equipment urgently needed in the active theaters of war, and hampering the organization of an effective defense against Allied landings.

The growing strength of the resistance forces was felt even more by Germany's Croatian and Italian allies, who had abandoned extensive areas of the countryside to the irregulars and restricted themselves to securing the larger centers of population and the main roads and rail lines. This withdrawal even permitted the organization by the Partisans of a provisional government in Bosnia.

The significance of these developments was not lost on the German Armed Forces High Command, which had issued a directive, over Hitler's signature on 28 December 1942, raising the status of the Armed Forces Commander, Southeast, to that of Commander-in-Chief, Southeast and his force to that of an army group.[4] General Loehr was enjoined, as Marshal List had been more than a year earlier, to establish adequate defenses against Allied landings, and to destroy all guerrilla groups in his rear, since they threatened the accomplishment of his mission.

---

[4] This redesignation of General Loehr's command as Army Group E, while his force was only that of an army, may also have been prompted by a desire to attain equal status in the Balkans area to that of the Italians. With their three armies, the Italians had organized an Army Group East headquarters in Tirana, Albania, and technically outranked Twelfth Army and the Armed Forces Commander, Southeast.

CHAPTER 7

OPERATIONS (JANUARY–AUGUST 1943)

I. Yugoslavia

It was evident that neither the Pavelitch government nor the Italian forces in Croatia could cope with the widespread activities of the Partisans. Accordingly, it devolved upon General Lueters, Commander of German Troops in Croatia, to take appropriate measures.

General Lueter's first large-scale action was Operation WEISS. This was to be executed in conjunction with Italian forces, with the mission of annihilating strong Partisan units in the mountainous region west and northwest of Sarajevo. The operation was to be completed in three phases, with Italian troops holding zone two on the Italian side of the demarcation line and allowing the Germans to move into zone three, evacuated some time previously and heavily infiltrated by the guerrillas.

The German force committed to WEISS included the 7th SS Mountain and 717th Infantry Divisions, the recently arrived 369th Infantry Division, and a regiment of the 187th Infantry Division. The Italian force was the V Corps of the Italian Second Army. In sharp fighting in the first phase of WEISS, the Germans and their allies inflicted more than 8,500 casualties on the Partisans, taking 2,010 prisoners. The German losses totalled 335 dead and 101 missing, with Croatian losses in proportion; Italian casualties were markedly lighter, since the Italian units lacked aggressiveness and the proper balance in heavy weapons to engage in sustained fire fights. WEISS I was concluded on 18 February, and the divisions immediately regrouped for the second phase, to be completed by mid-March.

Heavy fighting marked the opening of WEISS II. Additional troops of the VI Corps in Montenegro arrived to bolster the Italian force, but substantial numbers of Partisans managed to break through the Italian line and escape south and southeast into the wilder mountain regions of Hercegovina, Montenegro, and eastern Bosnia. Dispersing into almost inaccessible areas, the Partisan command group and numerous individuals managed to elude their pursuers. WEISS III, the Italian part of the operation, was completely unsuccessful.

WEISS was satisfactory from the German point of view in that the important bauxite-producing area of Yugoslavia was cleared of Partisans and heavy casualties were inflicted among them in the process. Moreover, the guerrillas were driven into barren and sparsely populated mountain areas offering little sustenance and few recruits to replace the battle losses.

The Chetniks became a matter of sharp contention between German and Italian commanders during the course of Operation WEISS. In fact, the Italians had been requested to disarm their Chetnik auxiliaries as part of WEISS III. However, regarded as allies by the Italians, many Chetnik units were supplied with arms and ammunition and given important missions in the conduct of operations.

Since repeated requests to disarm these Chetniks were met with evasion, local German commanders were instructed to disarm and detain as prisoners any Chetniks encountered in their areas of responsibility. Strong German protests to Mussolini finally had the desired effect, and the Italian field commanders were directed to cease delivery of arms and munitions to the Chetniks and to disarm them as soon as the Partisans had been destroyed.

To forestall any repetition of the events that made necessary such a large-scale undertaking as Operation WEISS, the German Armed Forces High Command directed the Commander-in-Chief, Southeast, to retain forces in that part of Croatia just cleared of the Partisans and to secure the bauxite mines in Dalmatia, in conjunction with the Italians. The commander of German forces in the Balkans was further directed to accelerate the organization of Croatian units and to keep the matter a secret from the Italians. Presumably, these measures would provide a large number of native troops to replace German units.

However, it soon became obvious that the situation would not be improved by such measures as the expansion of the demoralized Croat police and military forces. Large concentrations of Chetniks, including those supported by the Italians, formed a constant threat to German forces in the event of an Allied landing, and the Commander-in-Chief, Southeast, directed that Operation SCHWARZ, under the Commander of Troops in Croatia, be undertaken in May and June to destroy the Chetniks in Hercegovina and Montenegro.

In addition to the divisions he already had assigned to him, the Commander in Croatia received the 1st Mountain Division from the Russian front and a reinforced regimental combat team of the 104th Light Division from the German forces in Serbia for the projected operation.[5] Achieving surprise, the German forces inflicted heavy casualties on the Chetniks, capturing their commander in Montenegro, Major Djurisic, with 4,000 men, and forcing Mihailovitch to flee back into Serbia with the battered remnants of his command.

---

[5] The 704th, 714th, 717th, and 718th Infantry Divisions were reformed as light divisions in early 1943. Reference to them hereafter will be to the 104th, 114th, 117th, and 118th Light Divisions. Light divisions had an organization similar to that of the mountain divisions, but with additional motor transportation for employment on more level terrain.

There were also disorders in Serbia during this period. For the first three months of the year, 985 incidents were reported, including sabotage, attacks on native officials and police, and attacks on small German and Bulgarian troop units and installations. In a particularly unenviable position were the local officials, forced to remain in office by the Germans and regarded as collaborators by both Chetniks and Partisans. Fifty-eight were murdered during the first quarter of 1943, and 197 town halls were burned or damaged. In reprisal, in addition to burning some villages and levying fines in livestock, the occupation authorities ordered the shooting of several hundred hostages from among those arrested on suspicion of being members or supporters of the Chetnik and Partisan movements. These ruthless measures had the desired effect for a time, but could not prevent the regrouping of both Chetniks and Partisans as soon as the thinly spread German or Bulgarian forces had left a particular area.

Retaliation for attacks on the Bulgarian forces was even swifter, in many cases, than the reprisals meted out by the Germans. In one such incident, in March of 1943, 32 Bulgarians were killed and 26 wounded in an attack south of Skoplje. In their fury, the Bulgarian troops shot 288 persons in the vicinity, burned 550 houses, and placed 715 person under arrest. The readiness of the Bulgarians to shoot suspects without investigation of any kind finally prompted the German Commander in Serbia to request a careful preliminary examination of each case before an execution was carried out.

II. Greece

Receiving supplies and equipment by air through the 12 British liaison officers assigned by the British Middle East forces, the EDES organization had expanded from the 98 men with which it had commenced operations in 1942 to some 600 men two months later. This growth was accelerated by British broadcasts to Greece and the award of a high British decorataion to the EDES commander. The rapid growth of the force soon made it necessary to form a provisional battalion.

By March 1943, some 4,000 strong, EDES found it necessary to form more battalions and several regiments, some of which were commanded by former Greek Army officers. By July 1943, EDES had 8 to 10 units of two regiments each, the regiments each consisting of 2 battalions, and a total strength of 7,000 men. The headquarters and bulk of these forces were located in Epirus, and smaller groups operated in Thessaly and the Peloponnesus.

ELAS, leaderless until Sarafis assumed command in May 1943, was restricted to that time to a series of uncoordinated attacks. Under its new commander, however, ELAS soon emerged as an organized force.

With an estimated seven "divisions" and 12,000 men by mid-1943, ELAS units were active the length of Greece, with the exception of the Pindus Mountains area, held by EDES.

The initial successes of the guerrillas against the occupation forces in 1943 were brought to an abrupt end when the German 1st Mountain Division moved from Serbia into Greece and Albania in June to bolster the Italian effort. The guerrillas, with ample warning by their excellent intelligence system, planned a heavy blow against the new enemy before he could establish himself in his occupation role.

The guerrilla operation was to be launched as the mountain troops moved south through the village of Leskovic, high in the mountains along the Greek-Albanian frontier, on the Albanian side. (Map 4.) At that time, however, the border was crossed at will by local inhabitants, and the operation was primarily a Greek undertaking.

As was their custom, the guerrillas cleared the village of all inhabitants, then placed their own men in position in the buildings along the main street. Their plan was to allow the advance guard to pass, and then to fire on the main body when the troops were confined to the street and roadway. A large force of guerrillas would then emerge from hiding places in the hills nearby to complete the destruction of the demoralized Germans.

Instead of marching blindly into the village, however, the Germans first enveloped it from either flank, and a number of the guerrillas opened fire prematurely. Deploying rapidly, the main body of the mountain troops surrounded Leskovic and shelled it thoroughly before launching their assault. The guerrilla force in hiding outside the village was routed by artillery fire when it attempted to relieve the ambushers, and Leskovic was reduced in a house-to-house operation. The stone construction of the houses afforded considerable protection to the besieged guerrillas, who inflicted heavy casualties on the mountain troops before the latter could bring a sufficient number of infantry and antitank guns into action to batter down their positions.

A number of the irregulars escaped by posing as fleeing civilians while the battle was at its height. When the Germans recognized their opponents at close range, however, they halted everyone attempting to leave the village, and soon held a motley collection of ragged men and youths. Examinations of these prisoners and of the bodies found in the rubble of Leskovic revealed most of the guerrillas to have been in civilian clothing or parts of German and Italian uniforms, with their only insignia a small hammer and sickle. The aggressive attitude of the new occupation troops, with their heavier firepower and greater battle experience, soon discouraged such ventures as the attack at Leskovic, and for a time EDES also ceased all active operations against them. However, in deference to the British Middle East forces, Zervas could not openly accept the German offer of a truce. ELAS, on the other hand, persisted with small-scale attacks on individuals and small parties.

III. The German Situation by Mid-1943

With both Yugoslav and Greek guerrillas withdrawn from large-scale operations for the moment, the Germans hastened to take steps to secure the Balkans against a threatening Italian collapse or surrender. Arrangements were made to replace Italian garrisons with German troops, and German forces were disposed in locations from which they could move quickly to contest Allied landings. As directed by the new chief of the Supreme General Staff, Generale D'Armata (General) Vittorio Ambrosio, Italian units were to withdraw without delay, ostensibly for the defense of Italy against a threatening Anglo-American invasion. In many cases, Italian units left their assigned areas before the arrival of their German relief, and the Germans had to drive out infiltrating guerrillas before occupying their new positions.

Various expedients were attempted by the Germans in an effort to fill the power vacuum the Italian withdrawal was causing. One such measure was the westward extension of the Bulgarian occupation zones in Greece and Yugoslavia. However, the certain resentment of the population and the refusal of King Boris to move Bulgarian troops farther away from the Turkish-Bulgarian border made necessary the cancellation of these plans. Deeply concerned about the possibility of Turkey's entering the war on the Allied side, the Bulgarians kept idle major forces of first-line troops while sending second-rate divisions of older reservists to garrison their zones of Greece and Yugoslavia.

Nor was the reorganization of the Croat Army and security forces of any avail. Except for the Legion troops under German command, the Croatian military and security forces were confined to the larger centers of population. Desertions became more frequent, and even Legion troops could no longer be depended upon for missions not including a hard core of German units.

It was obvious that more German troops would be required if the Balkans were to be held. Temporarily, it would suffice to have satellite and puppet military and security forces hold the interior while German units moved to the coastal areas and likely invasion points. However, it would eventually be necessary to have reliable and combat-experienced troops to replace the puppet units or to furnish a cadre to stiffen them in operations. Accordingly, plans were made to strengthen the German forces by the induction of more ethnic Germans, by organizing several new divisions, and by bringing in a number of divisions and higher commands from other fronts and from German-occupied Europe.

By late June the 1st Panzer Division had arrived from France, where it had refitted after commitment on the northern and central Russian fronts. The newly formed LXVIII Corps headquarters, in army group reserve, was assigned the 1st Panzer and 117th Light Divisions, and given the mission of defending the Peloponnesus. Two other divisions were in the process of formation, the 100th Light Division in Croatia and the 297th Infantry Division in Serbia.[6] Additional Bulgarian troops also arrived, to bring the number of Bulgarian divisions in the occupied Balkans to seven.

As of the end of June, the Germans had a total of three Bulgarian one Italian, and 12 of their own divisions scattered throughout those areas of the Balkans under nominal German control. Several separate regiments and security battalions, the Russian Guard Corps, and a number of coastal defense battalions and supporting units were also available, though most were of limited combat potential. The Germans planned to commit their Croatian and Serbian puppet and security troops only in an auxiliary role.

The population of the areas held by the Germans, their weakening Italian allies, the Bulgarians, and the Pavelitch government totalled almost twenty-five million persons. In Greece, the occupiers wer opposed by ELAS and EDES forces estimated at 18,000 to 20,000 men in Yugoslavia by 50,000 to 60,000 Partisans, and 12,000 to 15,000 Chet niks (mobile units only); in Albania, by a total estimated to be a many as 20,000, with the strongest group that of the Communist leader Enver Hoxha.

Many excesses of the occupation troops, particularly of the Croa Ustascha, had alienated large segments of the population. Thi changing attitude was promptly exploited by the guerrilla leader: particularly the communists, who adopted a nationalist and popula front appeal to gain sympathy and support. Many former collabora tionists were forgiven and accepted into the guerrilla bands, thei ranks further swelled by Italian and Bulgarian deserters.

Eventual Allied victory had also become more obvious to the mas of the Balkan population by mid-1943, and few desired to be associate with a losing cause and reprisals. The judicious use of gold by th Allied liaison teams had brought a number of independent mountainee chieftains into the guerrilla camp, and the promise of weapons secure the loyalty of many clans in the more remote regions.

The successful Allied lodgment in Sicily on 10 July and the worser ing internal situation in the Balkans again raised the specter of enem landings along the Adriatic, on the Aegean islands, or against th western coast of Greece. Accordingly, the German Armed Force High Command, on 26 July, issued Directive No. 48, introducin

---

[6] Divisions originally bearing these numbers had been destroyed at Stalingrad.

major organizational changes and centralizing authority for the defense of the entire Balkan Peninsula. Generalfeldmarschall (Field Marshal) Maximilian von Weichs, formerly commander of Army Group B in southern Russia, became Commander-in-Chief, Southeast, replacing General Loehr, whose Army Group E was now restricted to Greece and the Greek islands. Marshal von Weichs, with headquarters at Belgrade, also directly commanded Army Group F, controlling all occupational troops in Yugoslavia and Albania.

One issue with the Italians was settled, at least temporarily, by the inclusion of the Italian Eleventh Army under the German theater command. In turn, the German LXVIII Corps, replacing the Italian VIII Corps on the Peloponnesus, came under control of Eleventh Army. Also, German forces in areas occupied by the Italians were placed under Italian command for tactical purposes.

Like similar directives issued earlier, the primary mission assigned the new Commander-in-Chief, Southeast, was to prepare the coastal defense of the Greek islands and mainland. To secure his rear area while so engaged and to prevent the disruption of his supply line and the movement of reinforcements in the event of Allied landings, he was further directed to destroy the guerrilla forces operating the length of the peninsula.

A mobile task force of 2 armored, 2 mountain, and 2 light infantry divisions was to be concentrated along the rail line south of Belgrade. In addition to securing the most sensitive section of the Belgrade–Athens line, this centrally located force would be available for commitment against any major beachhead the Allies might succeed in effecting.

The Bulgarian 7th Infantry Division in Thrace was attached to the German command at Salonika, and the Bulgarian corps would come under German control in the event of an Allied landing. All German civilian and government agencies, with the exception of the two chief representatives of the Foreign Office, also became subordinate to the Commander-in-Chief, Southeast.

Measures to effect a more thorough reorganization of the German forces in Greece and Yugoslavia and to complete the transposition of some headquarters from administrative (territorial) to tactical status followed Directive 48. The headquarters of the XXII Mountain Corps was formed from a part of the personnel from the headquarters of the Military Commander, Southern Greece; the functions of this area commander were absorbed by the new Military Commander, Greece, whose headquarters was formed from the remaining personnel. The headquarters in Serbia was disbanded, the personnel being used to form the headquarters of the XXI Mountain Corps, assigned to Albania, and the Military Command, Southeast. A third corps headquarters, the XV Mountain, was formed from personnel of the headquarters of the Commander of German Troops in Croatia; General Lueters assumed command of the new corps with many of his old staff.

Other corps headquarters formed at the time or moved into the area included the III SS Corps, V SS Mountain Corps, and the LI and LXIX Corps. One higher headquarters, that of Second Panzer Army, arrived from the Soviet Union and established its headquarters at Kragujevac, its mission to control the large mobile force to be formed in this central Balkan area south of Belgrade and to act as a mobile reserve to counter any Allied landings in force.

A number of small-scale operations were carried out against both Partisans and Chetniks throughout Yugoslavia during this period. In contrast to large-scale operations, these had the advantage of making easier the security of preparations and the achieving of surprise, and succeeded in keeping the irregulars constantly on the move. However, they had the disadvantage of allowing individual Partisans and Chetniks to slip through repeated encirclements and escape into areas recently combed by other units or where the occupation troops were not so active at the moment.

With the Italian ally about to join the enemy, the Commander-in-Chief, Southeast, was faced with the problem of holding extensive and rebellious areas with inadequate forces, while securing a long and exposed sea flank against an enemy having overwhelming naval and air superiority. Taking advantage of the situation, Partisan units became active in the Sarajevo area; in Albania, troops of the 100th Light Division had to be committed against guerrillas who had seized control of the Tirana airfield and were effectively blocking the landing of much-needed German reinforcements by air.

CHAPTER 8

THE DEFECTION OF ITALY AND ITS EFFECTS

I. General

Italian strength in Albania, Greece, and Yugoslavia comprised thirty-one division-sized units, the bulk of them under the Italian Army Group East in Tirana, and a total of 380,000 men at the time of the signing of the Italian armistice on 3 September 1943. Though in the process of withdrawing from the Balkans at the time their government capitulated and realined itself on the side of the Allies, these forces still held most of Albania; portions of Slovenia, Dalmatia, and Montenegro; the Ionian Coast and Islands of Greece; and a number of the Aegean Islands. In addition, they had troops in Croatia, in the interior of Greece, and under German command on Crete.

Negotiations between the Allies and the Badoglio government were conducted in great secrecy, thus the abrupt capitulation of Italy caught both Italian and German commanders by surprise. The immediate German reaction was to put Operation KONSTANTIN (seizing control of the Italian-occupied areas) into effect, and to disarm those Italian units that refused to continue the war on the German side. The capture of Foggia, with its great air base, and the adjacent ports in Italy by the Allies on 17 September made it imperative for the Germans to secure control of the Dalmatian coast and ports without delay. Unable to advance farther in Italy for the moment, the Allies might well attempt a crossing of the Adriatic in force.

The opportunity to procure much-needed weapons and equipment was not lost by the guerrillas, who immediately called upon the Italian garrisons to surrender. Fearful of guerrilla vengeance, however, many Italian units waited in place to be disarmed by the Germans, and the situation developed into a race between Germans and guerrillas to reach them.

II. Yugoslavia and Albania

Some 4,000 men of the Isonzo, Bergamo, and Zara Divisions in Dalmatia, Slovenia, and Croatia deserted their units to join the Partisans and Chetniks when the Italian armistice was announced. The Firenze Division, under its commander, went over as a unit to the guerrillas in Albania. A number of higher commanders and staffs managed to obtain transportation by air or sea to Italy, while the remaining Italian troops were disarmed by the Germans and guerrillas.

Incensed by what they considered treachery on the part of their former allies, the Germans made it a point to single out Italian units and installations in their continuing antiguerrilla operations. Italian troops disarmed by the irregulars were bombed and strafed in their unit areas by German airmen, and German ground troops hunted down Italian groups and units with the guerrilla forces opposing them.

The Dalmatian port of Split, with enormous stocks of food, clothing, fuel, and ammunition for the Italian occupation forces fell to the Partisans and their thousands of adherents among the dock workers and left-wing elements of the population. Though the Partisans were forced to evacuate Split, they managed to remove considerable quantities of stores before the arrival of German forces.

Nor were the Chetniks idle during this period of changing authority. Strong detachments moved into Dalmatia, seizing long stretches of the coastal areas and obtaining stocks of arms from Italian units sympathetic to them in the past.

The Croatian state, truncated by the Italian annexation of Dalmatia, moved forces into the coastal areas, fearing the Italians would try to hold Dalmatia until confirmed in its possession by the Allies as part of the reward for changing allegiance. Too, the *Poglavnik* had to impress his restless population, and a show of force against the former Italian overlords in their weakened state appeared to be an ideal opportunity.

The confused situation and sporadic fighting of the next few weeks ended with the Germans in control of the ports, main centers of population, and exposed coastal areas. The Partisans, laden with loot, were busily re-equipping and regrouping their forces in the mountains and carrying on a harrassing campaign against the new occupation troops. In Slovenia and Dalmatia, to relieve their own troops of many routine security duties, the Germans banded together the Italian-sponsored "White Guard" of Rupnik and the "Blue Guard" of Novak, the latter a Chetnik commander, into the "Domobran," a home guard type of organization.

Large numbers of Chetniks turned to the Partisans, and others gave up the struggle to return to their homes. The Croat units came under German control or returned to Croatia to support the weakening government of Ante Pavelitch.

III. Greece

Farther away from home than the troops in Yugoslavia, thousands of Italians in Greece chose to surrender to the Germans rather than the guerrillas. The Brennero Division declared itself ready to continue the war on the German side, and numerous Italian troops from other units were integrated into labor battalions. Unlike their countrymen in Yugoslavia, most of the remaining Italian troops in Greece were disarmed by the Germans and immediately interned.

Several major units, however, elected to aline themselves on the Allied side. The Pinerolo Division and Aosta Cavalry Regiment went over to the ELAS-EDES forces, and plans were made to commit them as units. When one proposed operation was refused by the Italians and another was completely unsuccessful, the Greeks disarmed both the division and the regiment and accepted volunteers from them into regular guerrilla units.

A few of the Italian troops in Greece managed to make their way back to Italy or fled to the mountains as individuals or in small groups, eventually to be captured by the guerrillas or to join the bands on their own initiative. A force of 1,100, war-weary and not desirous of fighting on either side, made its way to internment in neutral Turkey.

The situation on the Greek islands presented a different picture to that on the mainland. While Italian forces on Crete were disarmed without difficulty by the Germans, those on Rhodes surrendered only after a pitched battle and a strong show of force. On Cephalonia, the commander and 4,000 of the garrison were shot for resisting a German demand to surrender, and units on other islands established contact with British forces in the Middle East by radio to request reinforcements.

Augmented by British troops, the garrison of Leros held out against heavy German attacks for several months, finally surrendering with 5,350 Italians and 3,200 British on 17 November. Samos the last of the larger Greek islands held by the Italians, surrendered 5 days later.

It was proposed by some planners that the Germans abandon the southern part of the Balkan Peninsula and withdraw to a more defensible line in northern Greece. Hitler, however, would not permit it, nor could Germany risk exposing the sources of so many strategic raw materials to attack by aircraft the Allies would certainly bring with them to Greek bases. An estimated 50 percent of Germany's oil, all of its chrome, 60 percent of its bauxite, 24 percent of its antimony, and 21 percent of its copper were procured from Balkan sources. Hence, despite the advance of Allied troops in Italy to a point below Rome and the superiority of the Allied air forces over southern Greece and the Greek islands, the German defenders were ordered to remain in place.

CHAPTER 9

OPERATIONS TO THE END OF 1943

I. General

Exhausted by long marches and intermittent fighting to gain the areas vacated by the Italians, the German troops were in no condition to pursue the guerrillas into the mountains. Instead, German commanders hurried to set up a defense against Allied landings, allocated units specific areas of responsibility, and organized mobile forces to seek out and destroy the guerrilla bands.

Experience already gained in operations in the Balkans and in Russia enabled the Germans to devise more effective antiguerrilla measures than had their Italian predecessors. With the forces at hand, they set about to contain the guerrillas and keep up the flow of bauxite and other strategic raw materials produced in the Balkans to the German war machine.

On the passive defense side, the occupiers set up a network of *Stuetzpunkte* (strongpoints) to secure vital rail and road arteries and important installations. These strongpoints were actually small forts, heavily armed with automatic weapons, mortars, antitank guns, and even light field pieces, and situated in the vicinity of such guerrilla targets as bridges, tunnels, and portions of the rail and road lines difficult to keep under observation from the air or by roving patrols. Strongpoints were first occupied by a minimum of one squad, later by a platoon, when the smaller garrisons began to invite attack by the increasingly aggressive enemy. Some were of the field type, with earthen trenches and bunkers reinforced and revetted with logs and sandbags; others were elaborately constructed concrete fortifications with accommodations for a permanent garrison. They were situated to deliver all-round fire, and usually had radio communication with the next higher headquarters and adjacent strongpoints. Approaches to the positions were heavily mined, and the lanes through the mine fields were changed frequently. Barbed wire obstacles were also constructed, but were seldom effective against determined attackers.

Armored car patrols, a platoon or more in strength and equipped with searchlights and heavy weapons, made frequent and irregular runs between strongpoints; the same was done with armored trains along the vulnerable rail lines. In addition, mobile and heavily armed reserves were held on the alert at battalion and higher headquarters, ready to move immediately to the relief of strongpoints under attack.

Personnel limitations made it necessary to place strongpoints an average of 6 miles or more apart, requiring long patrols even on the main highways. The guerrillas were quick to take advantage of the situation and made extensive use of a pressure-type mine apparently supplied by the Western Allies or Russians. Disguised to resemble a stone, this mine had a nonmetallic casing and could not be discovered readily even with a mine detector. Placed on the rock-strewn mountain roads, the mine disabled numerous vehicles, leaving the German crews afoot and at the mercy of the roving guerrillas. Other devices put to extensive use were land mines, demolitions, and special nails designed to puncture tires. The last, easily transportable, could be dropped along the road at frequent intervals by shepherds moving their flocks from one grazing area to another.

A highly effective offensive weapon was found in the *Jagdkommando* (ranger detachment), designed to seek out and destroy guerrilla bands. Personnel of the detachments were usually young and combat-wise veterans of German campaigns on other fronts. Physically hardy and trained to live in the open for extended periods of time, they depended little on supply columns and could pursue the guerrillas, often burdened down with wounded, families, and impedimenta, into the most inaccessible areas. When the situation required, the rangers would put on civilian clothing, disguising themselves as Chetniks or Partisans, to work their way closer to their wary enemy. In the event they came upon major guerrilla forces, the ranger detachments, seldom more than a company in strength, would keep them under observation and inform battalion or other higher headquarters. While awaiting reinforcements, they would attempt to gather additional information on the guerrilla strength and dispositions. As successful as they were in many small-scale operations, however, the ranger detachments were not numerous enough to affect decisively the outcome of the antiguerrilla campaign.

A directive from the German Armed Forces High Command on 19 September made Generalfeldmarschall (Field Marshal) Rommel and Army Group B, in conjunction with the Commander-in-Chief, Southeast, responsible for destroying the large guerrilla forces on the Istrian Peninsula bordering Croatia.[7] Further, to strengthen the German Forces in the Balkans, the Commander-in-Chief, South, was to turn over to Marshal von Weichs all captured tanks and other armored

---

[7] Army Group B controlled operational and occupation forces in northern Italy until November, when it was replaced by Army Group C.

vehicles unsuitable for use against the Allies in Italy.[8] This ambitious plan to eliminate the guerrilla scourge in northwestern Yugoslavia and the Yugoslav-Italian border area, and a contemplated transfer of several divisions from Army Group B to the Commander-in-Chief, Southeast, was thwarted by developments in Italy and the departure of Marshal Rommel and his staff to France. Marshal von Weichs also lost the 1st Panzer Division, ordered to the Russian front in August.

German forces continued to move into the Balkans in the months following the defection of the Italians. By the end of September 1943, the number of German divisions had increased to 14. Total strength was approximately 600,000 military personnel, a serious drain on the Reich's dwindling manpower resources.[9] Opposing them, the Germans estimated the rapidly growing guerrilla forces in the theater at 145,000, the bulk of them, some 90,000, under Tito's command.

By early November the German forces in the Balkans comprised 17 divisions. The Armed Forces High Command then directed a search of all cities and centers of population in the Balkan Peninsula as a preliminary to major operations to destroy the guerrillas. Despite the strenuous objections of the theater commander, who protested the personnel available to him were far too few, the search operation was carried out on schedule, but with completely unsatisfactory results.

The Bulgarians also became a problem during November, with whole units disaffected by communist agitators. On one occasion, the 24th Bulgarian Division had to be withdrawn from an operation against the Partisans when it refused to obey the orders of the German task force commander. Desertions to the guerrillas became more frequent, and several communist bands of Bulgarian deserters were organized to operate against German forces and their own government in southern and western Bulgaria from bases on Yugoslav soil.

By the end of the year, German troop strength had climbed to 700,000 men, and a total of 20 infantry, SS, and mountain divisions. Despite this impressive total, however, and the attention the theater was receiving from the Armed Forces High Command, the southeast still held a secondary place in order of priority. Troop replacements were invariably older men or those returned to duty after long pe-

---

[8] The Commander-in-Chief, South, controlled all German forces in the Italian theater. The position at this time was held by Generalfeldmarschall (Field Marshal) Albert Kesselring.

[9] This figure includes labor and administrative troops of all types. Also, at the time, there were an assault gun brigade, several regiments of security troops, a motorized infantry regiment, (reinforced) and a number of security and fortress battalions of army group troops.

riods in the hospital. Vehicles, including tanks, were often obsolescent or war booty from the 1940 campaign in western Europe. (Chart 3.)

II. Yugoslavia and Albania

Major anti-Partisan operations planned for late 1943 included KUGELBLITZ, SCHNEESTURM, and HERBSTGEWITTER. The first of these, executed by the V SS Mountain Corps, had as its purpose the destruction of the Partisan units in eastern Bosnia. The German troop units had to comb too large an area to be thorough, however, and the bulk of the Partisan force slipped through their narrowing ring. The Partisans suffered 9,000 casualties in the course of the operation, and were immediately pursued in Operation SCHNEESTURM, twin drives to the west and northwest. Concluded by the end of December, SCHNEESTURM cost the Partisans an additional 2,000 men. Though badly battered in these operations, the major Partisan units retained their cohesion and Tito's Army of National Liberation could still be considered an effective fighting force.

HERBSTGEWITTER involved the clearing of the island of Korcula, off the Dalmatian Coast, an excellent waystation for bringing supplies in by sea from Italy. The Partisans lost 1,000 men in the operation. However, perhaps more significant than this loss was the matter of a reprisal inflicted on the Partisan garrison. The Commander-in-Chief, Southeast, had received a report on the shooting of 3 German officers and 26 enlisted men captured by the 29th Partisan Division near Mostar. (Map 3.) One of the officers was a holder of the Knight's Cross of the Iron Cross (the German equivalent of the Distinguished Service Cross), which further incensed Marshal von Weichs. Accordingly, he ordered the execution of 220 prisoners from Korcula in reprisal, giving the Partisans additional ammunition for their propaganda campaign.

As of the end of the year, the headquarters of Second Panzer Army, which had arrived from Russia in August to assume control of the major striking force of Army Group F, had 14 divisions in Yugoslavia and Albania. The 367th Infantry Division, hastily formed in Germany in October, was assigned to garrison duty in Croatia while completing its organization and training. The Military Command, Southeast, had operational control over the I Bulgarian Corps in Serbia and a number of police and security units of regimental and battalion size.

It was at this time that a number of the Allied liaison officers were withdrawn from the Chetniks, and with their departure the supply of weapons and equipment from the Middle East forces and Italy was considerably reduced. With much of their portion of Allied military

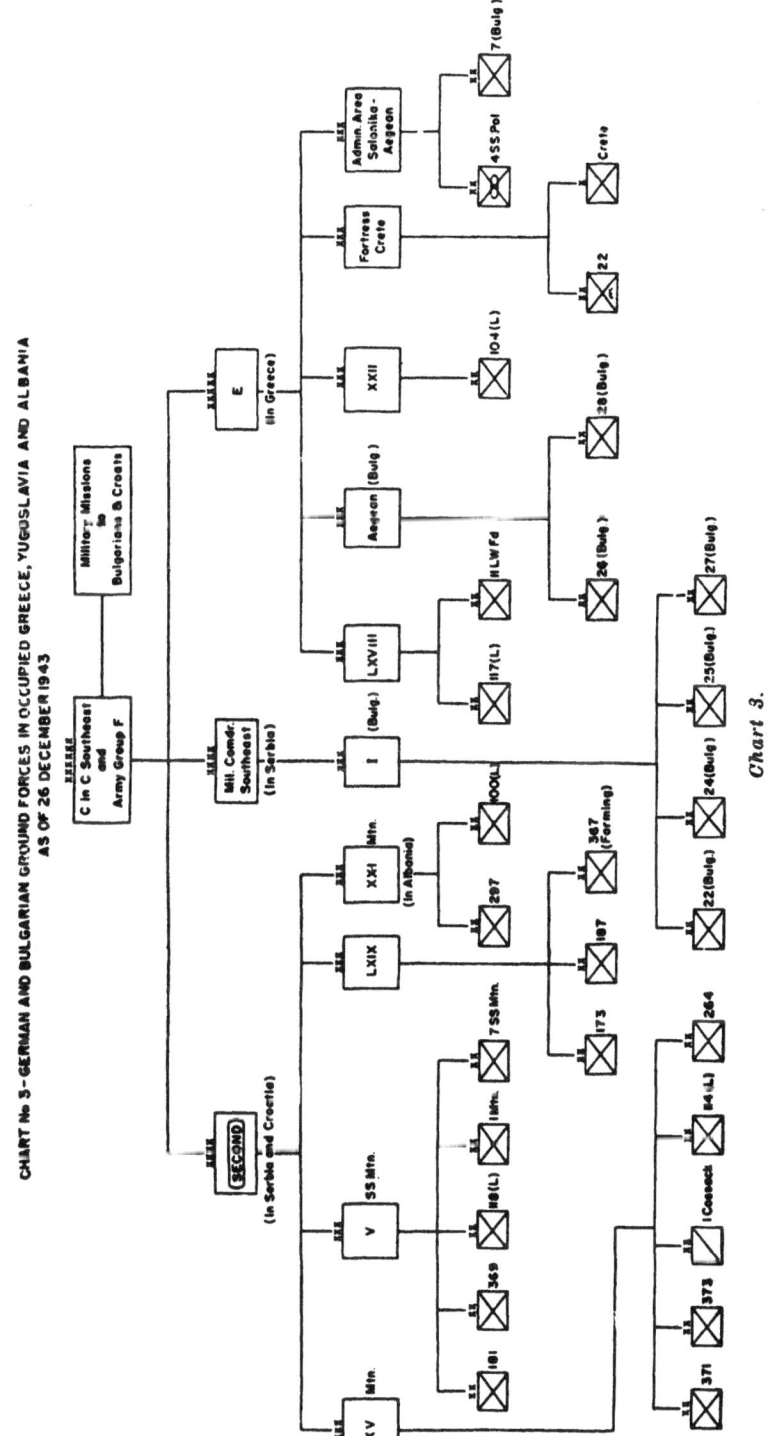

Chart 3.

assistance diverted to the Partisans and under constant attack by Tito's forces, the position of the Chetniks began to deteriorate. Though they still held Serbia and some of the Adriatic coastal regions, their strength waned with battle losses and desertions.

No doubt existed as to the loyalty of Mihailovitch himself to the royal Yugoslav Government-in-Exile. However, there is ample evidence that a number of his subordinates made armistice arrangements with the occupation forces and even assisted them on occasion. Certain the Germans and their allies would eventually be forced to withdraw from the Balkans, Mihailovitch regarded the Partisans, under the aegis of Moscow, as the greater of the two threats to the restoration of the former government.

III. Greece

With its more homogeneous population and a central government, however weak and collaborationist, Greece did not pose the occupation problem that Yugoslavia did during this period. The average German had considerable respect for the culture of ancient Hellas, and was better disposed toward the Greek population than toward the various Yugoslav peoples, whom he regarded as offshoots of the Russians and Slavic barbarians. Too, the economic situation in Greece, unable to raise enough food to sustain even its own population and reduced to abject poverty by the complete loss of its world-wide foreign trade of prewar years, did much to keep the Greeks under the control of the occupation forces and the puppet regime.

Major operations undertaken by the Germans during the period were the clearing of the Edessa–Florina road, west of Salonika, accomplished in conjunction with Bulgarian forces moved west for the purpose, and PANTHER, the elimination of guerrilla bands in the Metsovan Pass, Yannina–Arta, and Mount Olympus areas. (Map 4.) In the Edessa-Florina operation, the guerrilla forces melted away into the mountains, and neither side sustained casualties comparable to those suffered in the fighting in Yugoslavia. In Operation PANTHER, the guerrillas lost 1,400 men, 3 field pieces, and a considererable stock of small arms.

As of the end of the year, Army Group E had attached to it the XXII Mountain and LXVIII Corps, the former responsible for western Greece and the Peloponnesus and the latter for eastern Greece. In addition, Fortress Crete, raised to corps status and no longer under the theater headquarters, was directly responsible to the army group commander. A total of 6 divisions, 1 of them Bulgarian, formed the combat nucleus of the army group. In the event of major Allied landings, the 2 divisions from the Bulgarian corps in Thrace would also come under the control of Army Group E.

MAP 4.—German dispositions

CHAPTER 10
OPERATIONS IN 1944

I. General

The Italians had been eliminated from a major role on the military scene, except for individuals and small units fighting on either side, and the Balkan occupation by the beginning of 1944 had become a heavy burden to the Germans. The Wehrmacht was bleeding to death in Russia, and the invasion of France was but a few months away; United States, British, and other Allied forces were firmly established in Italy. The Bulgarians, formerly reliable allies and assigned a responsible part in the occupation, were growing acutely concerned with the possibility of Turkey's entering the war on the Allied side; a Turkish attack through Thrace had become a nightmare to the Bulgarian leaders.

The lesser satellite and puppet forces, including the Ustascha and national army of Croatia, the Serbian State Guard and Volunteer Corps, and various Yugoslav, Greek, and Albanian security and auxiliary units, had begun to desert in increasing numbers to the Partisans and ELAS, and a few to the Chetniks and EDES. The Russian Guard Corps, as well as such Russian-German formations as the 1st Cossack Division, which had arrived in Yugoslavia in late 1943, remained loyal to the Germans. However, the dilution of the Guard Corps with former prisoners of war and the excesses of the Cossack Division against the civilian population reacted to the disadvantage of the Germans. The former prisoners, brought up in the Soviet mold, were completely alien to the older Russians, and the Guard Corps lost some of its Czarist flavor. The 1st Cossack Division, which included Kuban, Terek, Don, and Siberian Cossacks who had seen hard service against Soviet guerrillas, left a trail of burned villages and terror-stricken peasants in its wake.

The German units, however, despite this weakened support, still presented a formidable military force to the irregulars, and could march into and occupy any part of Greece, Albania, and Yugoslavia at any time, an argument often given to justify their treatment of captured guerrillas as illegal combatants. Moreover, strong and seasoned reserves were available in the 1st Mountain Division, as well as several others less well known, to be rushed to the scene of any protracted rising. (Map 4.)

II. The Area of Army Group E

To keep as many as possible of its better-trained troops available as a mobile striking force to counter Allied landings in Greece, Army Group E had already received a number of "Eastern" battalions, composed of Russians, Ukranians, Poles, and other Slavic groups, to supplement its German security units. Too, thousands of Italians, after a few months in German internment camps, found a more tolerable existence in labor and other auxiliary units. Known to the Germans as *Hiwis* (*Hilfswillige*), the labor troops relieved combat units by building coastal fortifications, constructing strongpoints, and repairing the extensive damage done by Allied bombing, now increasing in intensity; the *Kawis* (*Kampfwillige*) assisted by performing various guard and security duties. The heterogeneous collection of foreign troops proved insufficient for the maintenance of law and order in Greece, however, and the commander of Army Group E requested and received permission to raise and equip a battalion of Greek security troops, knowing approval for more would be forthcoming if the new unit could make any substantial contribution to the German defense plan.

This pilot model was known as the Laocoon Volunteer Battalion, after Laocoon of Greek mythology, and had approximately 700 men. Arms were limited to rifles and machine guns, and the first mission of the battalion was to participate in the clearing of the Peloponnesus. The fair success attained in the operation convinced the Germans of the advisability of organizing two additional battalions.

The practice of replacing German units with foreign troops had its disadvantages, however. For example, it had become necessary for General Loehr to warn all Russian members of the Eastern battalions against desertion. The worsening German war situation had prompted Stalin to call on all Soviet citizens in German service to obstruct operations in any way they could, and a number had done so by deserting, spreading rumors, and inciting the troops against their German officers and noncommissioned officers.

Next, the general reluctance among the Italians in the German auxiliary services caused the army group commander to require an oath of allegiance from each man. A full 30 percent of the Italians refused to take the oath, and rumors were rife among the 70 percent who did that they would be called upon for front-line service. According to other rumors, each man taking the oath of allegiance in the German cause would be imprisoned for 10 years if he were ever to return to Italy. The already low morale and lukewarm support of the Italians sank to new depths when this news became general knowledge among the labor and security units.

Nor had the situation with the Bulgarians improved. Reports from the liaison officer with the II Bulgarian Corps stressed the defeatist attitude of the corps commander and his staff, who despaired of holding the Thracian coast against a determined Anglo-American landing in force.[10] Rather, the Bulgarians preferred to build a defense line along the Rhodope Mountains, just inside their own country. Believing an invasion would be preceded by a large-scale airborne landing to their rear, they feared the cutting of communications with the Bulgarian zone of the interior.

Respecting the Bulgarians as hardy and willing soldiers, the Germans pointed out that the Bulgarian lack of experience in modern military operations had caused them to overestimate the Allies, and that a strong coastal defense organization would discourage any landing in an area so exposed to a German flank attack from the Greek peninsula. The Bulgarians, temporarily reassured, expanded their construction of coastal defenses and agreed to send a number of their commanders and staff officers to observe German operations in Italy.

The German units, bearing the brunt of the antiguerrilla effort, had difficulties of their own, chief among them a shortage of personnel. To supplement the trickle of replacements, General Loehr directed all service organizations to make their able-bodied men available for transfer to combat units. The commander of Army Group E also had to overcome some lethargy on the part of subordinate headquarters, and on one occasion sent a sternly worded directive ordering the abolishment of such terms as "Sunday duty" from the staff duty rosters of the corps and area commands.

A number of operations were undertaken by units of Army Group E during the opening months of 1944 in an attempt to clear guerrilla-infested areas of Greece. Though not on the large scale of operations in Yugoslavia to the north, they nonetheless diverted thousands of troops from the preparation of coastal defenses and transfer to other theaters of war. In addition, they involved extensive use of vehicles and an expenditure of gasoline the Germans could ill afford.

The first operation of significance, in the Salonika-Aegean area, was called WOLF; both German and Bulgarian troops participated. A total of 254 enemy dead was counted, and over 400 prisoners taken. Operation HORRIDO followed, with units of the XXII Mountain Corps participating. Guerrilla casualties totalled 310 dead and 15 captured, while the German troops suffered 18 dead, wounded, and missing.

During this period the economic situation worsened steadily, with the value of the Greek drachma reduced to a point where it required 500,000 to purchase a pound of butter on the widespread black market. As a result, large numbers of Greeks fled to join the guerrillas, particularly the communist group. General Loehr, for this reason, found it

---

[10] The headquarters of the Bulgarian II Corps replaced the headquarters of the Bulgarian Aegean Corps in control of the divisions in Thrace at the turn of the year.

necessary to direct the troops to desist from interfering with food shipments and neutral relief agencies, in the hope the gap in security his order created would be offset by an improved level of subsistence for the bulk of the population.

The Germans still had some supporters from the anticommunist elements of the Greek population, among them EDES. For keeping the Yannina—Arta road and a large part of the Pindus Mountains area cleared of ELAS forces, EDES was supplied with small arms and ammunition by local German commanders, a practice approved by the army group commander. According to revised German estimates, Zervas' main force at this time comprised only 2,500–3,000 men, but these were well disciplined, adequately armed, and organized into properly balanced units, with sufficient heavy weapons for support in their particular type of combat. ELAS, by contrast, had grown to 20,000 men, uniformly armed only to battalion and lacking heavy weapons in sufficient numbers or the more rigid organization and discipline of Zervas' nationalists.

Started the end of February, Operation RENNTIER was concluded in March, with a total of 96 guerrilla dead and 100 prisoners. The Germans suffered 2 and the Bulgarians 7 casualties in the operation. A second operation in the Salonika-Aegean area, with the code name ILTIS, cost the guerrillas an additional 15 men.

A communist-inspired strike in the Piraeus area in March was put down by the Germans only after security troops fired on the demonstrators, killing 21; an additional 132 strikers were taken into custody. Immediately following this, a German truck column on the Sparta–Tripolis road in the Peloponnesus was attacked, and a total of 18 Germans killed and 44 wounded. In reprisal, 200 communist suspects were executed, 10 villages burned, and martial law declared throughout the Peloponnesus. Both of these events worsened relations between the Greek civilian population and the German occupiers.

Another measure taken by Army Group E was the establishment of a restricted zone on either side of the railroad lines used by the German forces. In open country, this extended to 5 kilometers (approx. 3 miles) on either side of the track; in populated areas, to 200 meters (220 yds.). Within this zone, civilians were warned, they would be fired upon on sight.

While clearing operations, restrictions on movement in the area of the rail lines, and the active assistance of EDES and the Greek volunteer battalions restored a measure of security to the German supply routes, guerrilla forces increased their activities in more remote areas. On Euboea, elements of the LXVIII Corps and Greek auxiliaries had to be committed in a clearing operation that cost the guerrillas 85 dead and 69 prisoners. A concurrent small-scale operation in the Salonika-Aegean area cost the Greek resistance forces 13 casualties and the Germans 12. Continuously engaged in operations, the occupational command for the Salonika-Aegean area became the Salonika Corps Group, and was raised to tactical corps status.

Friction again developed with the Bulgarians at this time. Contrary to the wishes of the Germans, to whom they were now subordinated tactically, the Bulgarians assigned fully a quarter of the troops of their II Corps to the task of securing the interior of Thrace, up to the mountain passes into Bulgaria. The Germans protested this weakening of the coastal garrisons, already reduced to a point where only 11 heavy batteries were left available for coast artillery support for an exposed sea front of almost 200 miles. In reply, the Bulgarians stated they considered it necessary to secure a route for reinforcements in the event of an Allied landing.

Despite the dissatisfaction of Army Group E, the Bulgarians maintained their position, widening the breach in relations. The irritation grew with some activities of Bulgarian units operating in German-occupied areas. Reluctant to leave after the completion of a mission, the Bulgarians frequently had to be ordered to return to their own zone. In turn, these units resented the German requirement that they turn over all weapons and booty taken in joint operations. Bulgarian minorities in German-occupied Greece also played a part in the dissension. Allowed to form home guard-type companies at the insistence of the Bulgarian II Corps, the minorities used these armed units to dominate their Greek neighbors, who in turn blamed the German authorities for placing them in such a position.

Operations in early April involved the clearing of a number of mountain passes in northern Greece, a preliminary movement to Operation MAIGEWITTER, a large-scale effort to destroy ELAS forces in that part of the army group area. The total guerrilla loss in the operation was 339 dead and 75 captured, with 200 suspects arrested.

Repeated Allied commando and air raids on the Greek islands made necessary the issuance of special instructions to the captains of the small vessels making the hazardous supply runs to isolated garrisons in the Aegean and Ionian Seas areas. Gun crews were to stand by at action stations when their vessels approached island anchorages, and supplies were to be unloaded only after the garrisons had been identified. Movement was to be at night where possible, with gun crews ready for sudden air attacks even in port. The excellent intelligence net of the guerrillas and Allies made it difficult for the Germans to maintain security of ship movements, however; this was well illustrated by the sinking of a ship carrying large stocks of small arms and machine gun ammunition to Crete and other island outposts.

On several occasions British commando troops managed to remain on various Greek islands for periods of several days, making detailed reconnaissance and taking prisoners for interrogation at Middle East headquarters. Perhaps the best known of these prisoners was Generalmajor (Brigadier General) Karl Kreipe, commanding the 22d Airborne Division on Crete, and captured on 26 April by a party that penetrated the coastal defenses and succeeded in evacuating the general past a number of security outposts. This persistent Allied interest in Greece tended to keep the German occupying forces constantly on the alert, a strain on commanders, staffs, troops, and communications. The mounting number of suicides on Crete alone, from 11 in 1942 to 41 in 1943, perhaps best exemplified the slump in morale and spirit occasioned by this type of duty. The garrison of Crete was evacuated before the end of 1944, hence no figures are available for that year. However, the situation became serious enough to be called to the attention of General Loehr by his chief medical officer.

The situation in Greece became more tense during May and June. The army group commander, to provide additional armed men in the event of emergency, directed the conscription of all able-bodied, male Germans resident in Greece, including civilians attached to the economic and diplomatic missions, the Organization Todt (construction workers), and employees of the various armed services. Practice alerts were held frequently, and rear area troops, as well as the provisional units of new conscripts, were given intensive instruction in the use of small arms.

The guerrillas, meanwhile, emboldened by the prospect of an impending German withdrawal, increased the tempo of their attacks. During the first week of May, Generalleutnant (Major General) Krech, commanding the 41st Fortress Division on the Peloponnesus, was killed in a surprise attack, with 3 enlisted men of his headquarters; 325 communist suspects were shot in reprisal. Other attacks were made on German supply lines, and sabotage extended even to armed vessels at anchor in Greek harbors.

Apparently oblivious to the situation in which the German forces in Greece now found themselves, the Armed Forces High Command, through the headquarters of Marshal von Weichs, directed the securing of the Greek sea areas and the defense of the peninsula to the last. Operation NEPTUN, later compromised and changed to KORALLE, was undertaken to clear the Sporades Islands area and adjacent waters in compliance with this order, but succeeded only in drawing superior British naval forces to the scene of battle. EINHORN, also compromised and changed to GEMSBOCK, was completed by the XXII Mountain Corps in early June; the purpose of the operation was to inflict a decisive defeat on the growing guerrilla forces in the Greek-

Albanian border area. Quite successful, GEMSBOCK was followed three weeks later by Operation STEINADLER, to destroy ELAS units in the Pentalofon area.[11]

While the XXII Mountain Corps conducted GEMSBOCK in western Greece and southern Albania, the LXVIII Corps in the Peloponnesus and eastern Greece pursued several operations of its own. The results in the numbers of guerrillas killed and captured, however, were considerably less than in GEMSBOCK.

An increasing number of desertions by the Ossets, a Caucasus Mountains race well represented in the Eastern battalions, caused the army group commander to direct that all Ossets be disarmed and detained as prisoners of war. From a support to German manpower, the "Eastern" battalions now became an increasing liability. A watch also had to be kept on the Italian volunteers dispersed throughout the German security battalions in a ratio of one "company" of 40 men per battalion. Reports of disaffection among such units under German command in northern Italy caused considerable concern over the matter at army group headquarters. A number of Bulgarian volunteers serving in Wehrmacht units also had to be disarmed in June, as did part of the 814th Armenian Battalion, adding to the enormous number of prisoners of war and internees in German custody in Greece.

Early July brought a realinement of German combat strength in Greece when the 4th SS Police Division, which had then been in Greece almost a year, was alerted for movement to the north. The consequent shifting of forces made it necessary for the 41st Fortress Division, a static unit composed in large part of former general military prisoners, to take over the defense of the entire Peloponnesus. The 11th Luftwaffe Field Division, in Attica, was given an added area of responsibility, which included Thessaly, infested by ELAS and EKKA forces. Units of the air force field division lost control of much of the area to the guerrillas in a matter of days, and had difficulty maintaining the major north-south roads and rail lines.

On 3 July EDES abruptly reopened hostilities with the occupation forces, seizing 10 kilometers (6½ miles) of coastline in the vicinity of Parga. (Map 4.) Two days later, during the night of 5–6 July, EDES forces attacked German troops in the vicinity of Arta. To defend themselves, the Germans undertook several small-scale countermoves, meanwhile trying to determine the intentions of Zervas prior to any major offensive to eliminate him. Intelligence reports at first supported the theory that British liaison officers had seized command of the Zervas organization, in conjunction with a group

---

[11] For a detailed discussion of Operations GEMSBOCK and STEINADLER, see Chapter 11.

of anti-German commanders led by Colonel Kamaras of the 10th EDES Division. Later, several clandestine meetings between Zervas and representatives of the German forces made it obvious that the Greek leader had been influenced by the Allied liaison mission to renege on his agreement with the occupation forces. The coastal area Zervas had seized, with its easy access to the EDES-controlled Pindus Mountains, permitted the landing of 5,000 reinforcements from the Greek units under British command in Egypt. These units were immediately distributed throughout the Zervas organization and represented a substantial increase in effective troop strength. (Map 5.)

Since a reinforced and hostile EDES represented a threat to his forces, the commander of Army Group E directed the destruction of the Zervas organization after the completion of Operation STEINADLER. General Loehr also directed additional changes in coastal defense, based on German experiences in the Normandy operation. Beach defenses were to be manned only by troops of the static fortress battalions, while the reduced mobile forces of the 104th Light and other divisions were to be assembled in areas to the rear to counter Allied landings.

The offensive against EDES, for which the already alerted 4th SS Division was made available, was the responsibility of the XXII Mountain Corps. Called by the code name of KREUZOTTER, the operation, beginning 5 August, was only moderately successful. EDES lost a total of 298 dead and 260 prisoners, as against German casualties of 20 dead, 112 wounded, and one missing.

More important events, on the international scene, soon eclipsed antiguerrilla operations in the area of Army Group E. The Romanians surrendered to the advancing Russians on 24 August, and Soviet forces were perilously close to the Bulgarian frontier. Though not at war with the Soviet Union, the Bulgarians feared imminent invasion by either Russians or Turks, and government leaders met to consider ending the alliance with Germany. As a result, orders were given Bulgarian frontier troops to disarm German units withdrawing from Romania, and the II Corps, in Thrace, was directed to prepare for movement home during the first week in September. The German liaison missions with higher Bulgarian headquarters remained on in their assignments, however, and Wehrmacht units scattered throughout Thrace and in Bulgaria itself organized themselves into small combat groups to resist any attempt by the Bulgarians to disarm them. Hitler, furious at what he considered Bulgarian duplicity, ordered all German troops moving into Bulgaria to remain under arms and all units to defend their positions in Bulgaria and Bulgarian-occupied areas to the last cartridge (an order now somewhat timeworn in the Fuehrer's directives to his field commanders).

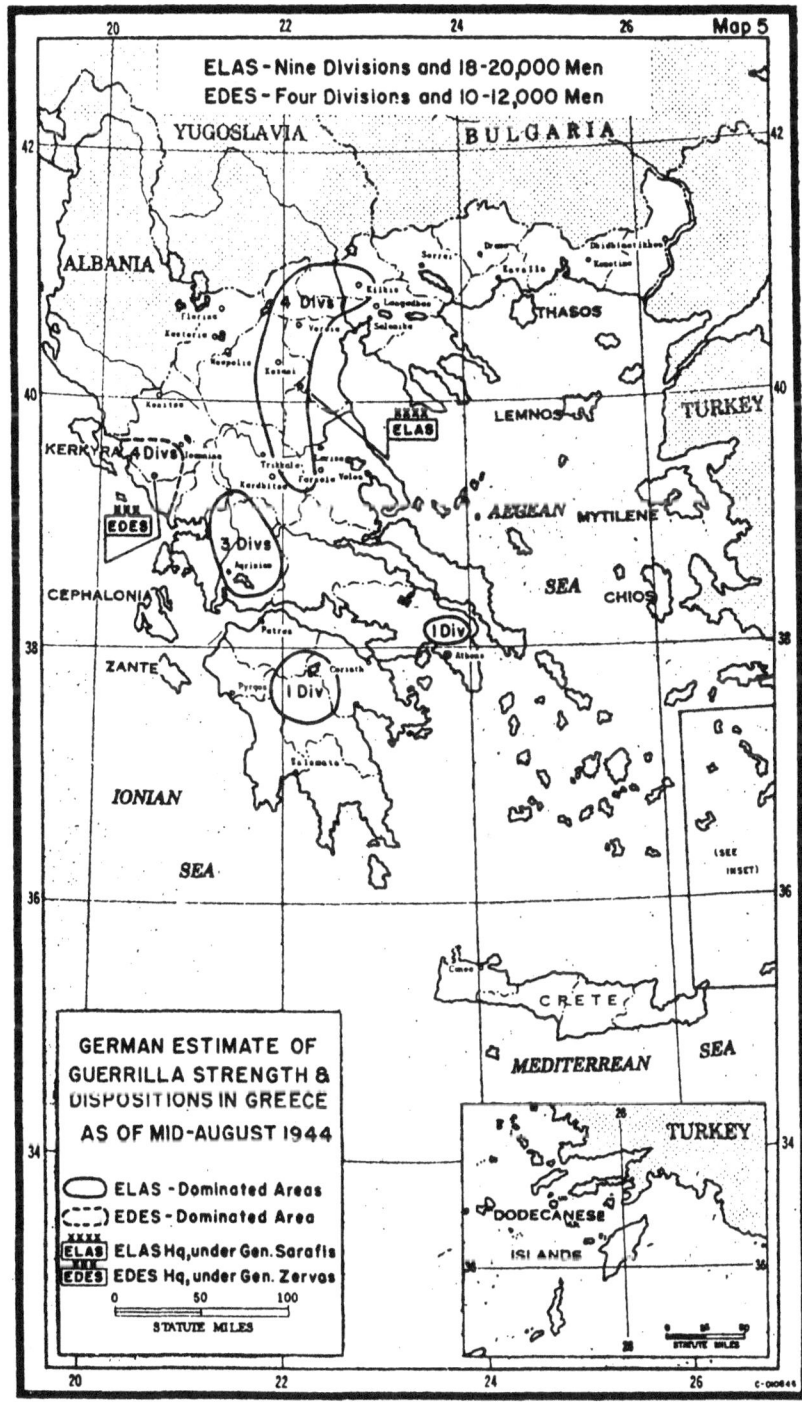

Map 5. German estimate of guerrilla strength and dispositions in Greece as of mid-August 1944.

Among the troops and commanders, German-Bulgarian relations remained amicable enough. In evacuating the coastal area, Bulgarian artillery units left their immobile pieces in position for German crews to man, and the German liaison officer to the II Corps was allowed to maintain contact with the headquarters of Army Group E. Individuals and small parties outside their respective zones were allowed to return to their units unmolested.

While resigned to the loss of Thrace, the Bulgarian Government, despite the imminent crisis with the Soviet Union, had no intention of relinquishing its status in Yugoslavia. Accordingly, since it lay directly across the main axis of communications between Army Group E and German headquarters for all the southeast at Belgrade, it was necessary for the Germans to make plans to secure Yugoslav Macedonia and southeastern Serbia, the former occupied by the Bulgarian V Corps and the latter by the I Corps. Plan TREUBRUCH assigned the 1st Mountain Division the mission of seizing Skoplje, largest city and rail center of the area; Plan HUNDESSOHN involved the movement of the 4th SS Police Division into Bulgaria in the direction of Sofiya, the capital; Plan JUDAS was the disarmament of the Bulgarian forces in Thrace and Macedonia. Arrangements were made with Army Group F for units of Army Group E to move into its area of responsibility.

While German units prepared for their respective parts in the operations planned in event of hostilities with Bulgaria, fighting with the guerrilla forces increased in intensity. For the 2-month period ending in August, the Germans suffered a total of 936 dead, 1,235 wounded, and 275 missing, meanwhile inflicting casualties on the guerrillas amount to 5,394 dead and 768 captured. Personnel casualties in air attacks on trains, convoys, and troop areas also reached a high during this period, with 32 dead and 26 wounded for the week ending 4 August alone. To improve the air defense of their rail lines and installations, Luftwaffe units were directed to fly high over the railroads and to avoid flying parallel to them. Antiaircraft crews and troops defending the trains and lines were then free to open fire on any aircraft approaching at a low altitude.

The situation by the end of August made it necessary for Army Group E to order the evacuation of all troops in Greece, with the exception of the garrisons of Crete and Rhodes, to the area north of the line Corfu-Yannina-Kalabaka-Olympus. The withdrawal was to be orderly, and measures taken to prevent German intentions becoming known to the Greek population. The troops on railroad security duty were reinforced, and Corps Group Salonika, a provisional organization formed from the administrative command for the Salonika-Aegean area, was merged with an existing skeletal staff to form the

XCI Corps headquarters and control units in the Salonika region, through which all forces from the south would have to pass.

On 8 September, Bulgaria declared war on Germany and immediately dispatched strong forces from Sofiya in the direction of the Yugoslav frontier. Lacking the strength to put their ambitious HUNDESSOHN and JUDAS plans into effect, the Germans hurried the 1st Mountain Division to Skoplje, where it operated temporarily under control of the Second Panzer Army, to implement Plan TREUBRUCH. While 5,000 Bulgarians at Bitolj laid down their arms after a brief show of resistance, the garrison at Prilep and Bulgarian units in the Skoplje area fought stubbornly. However, the 1st Mountain Division eventually managed to seize and hold the city of Skoplje and the vital railroad along the Vardar River. Bulgarian units bypassed in the fast German move to the north succeeded in breaking the line at a number of points and had to be driven off by combat groups formed from troops moving northward from Greece to join the 1st Mountain Division.

On the night of 8–9 September, a general rising made it obvious that German units below the line Corfu–Yannina–Kalabaka–Olympus would have to fight their way north. Moving down from the mountains in force, both ELAS and EDES attempted to block the major roads and railways to the north. In western Greece, troops of the XXII Mountain Corps had to fight hard to keep the Arta–Yannina road open in order to evacuate the Cephalonia garrison and units in southwestern Greece. In eastern Greece, the LXVIII Reserve Corps, having already lost its 11th Luftwaffe Field Division to the defense of Macedonia, managed to regain long stretches of the rail line to Salonika only after a series of seesaw actions with strong ELAS units.

To reinforce the units already heavily engaged in the north and threatened by an estimated three Bulgarian armies moving west to cut off the withdrawal of Army Group E, General Loehr directed an airlift of combat troops from Crete and Rhodes. A total of 11,500 men evacuated from Crete alone in this operation, most of them from the 22d Airborne Division, proved to be a substantial addition to the hard-pressed units north of Salonika. However, fighter aircraft from Allied carriers now operating in force in Greek waters made impossible the completion of the airlift. As of 12 October, some 26,500 service and combat troops were still stranded on Crete, Rhodes, and other German-held islands, with little or no prospect of escape. Instructed to fight to the end and destroy all installations and materiel of value to the enemy, the bulk of these troops, representing all three services, were left to their fate.

Its success in holding open the route of withdrawal to the north could not obscure the fact that Army Group E was in a difficult position. All available troops had been thrown into the fighting against the Russians and Bulgarians along a line roughly paralleling the southeastern Yugoslav border. In the rear areas in Yugoslav Macedonia, Albanian guerrillas and Partisan units roamed almost at will off the main roads and rail lines, and the Partisans had established contact with Bulgarian irregulars operating with their own army as reconnaissance and screening forces. Accordingly, Army Group E directed the complete evacuation of Greece and the establishment of a new defense along the line Scutari–Skoplje–Negotin. (Map 4.) On 14 October headquarters of Army Group E moved to Yugoslav Macedonia, where it estimated it had the equivalent of four German divisions holding a line of 375 miles against $13\frac{1}{2}$ Soviet and Bulgarian divisions. While the rugged country allowed them to confine their efforts to holding the mountain passes and other avenues of approach, this advantage was more than offset by the German inferiority in numbers and lack of air support and by the activities of the guerrillas. Information from prisoners revealed the Third Ukrainian Front (Army Group) to be in Sofiya directing operations, with the Thirty Seventh and Fifty Seventh Soviet Armies under its control. The Bulgarian armies were the First, Second, and Fourth. The use of Stuka aircraft by the Bulgarians, who had obtained them under the Axis equivalent of lend-lease during the period of the alliance with Germany, was particularly exasperating to the troops of Army Group E.

The few units still remaining in Greece, comprising mostly supply and other service troops, now found themselves in a position similar to that of the island garrisons. Lacking adequate transportation and the fire-power of combat units, these troops were ordered to fight to the last and to destroy all stocks and equipment of any value to the guerrillas. While some carried out the destruction as ordered, in a number of cases installation commanders turned critically needed food, medicines, and clothing over to agencies of the Greek Government.

As British troops landed in southern Greece and the occupation rapidly approached its end, ELAS and EDES became engaged in a civil war that prevented both them and the British from participating in the pursuit of the Germans. On 2 November the last organized German units to evacuate Greece crossed the border into Yugoslavia, and German control of Greece was history.

III. The Area of Army Group F

The German command structure in Yugoslavia as of the first of the year was an anomaly. Army Group F, which controlled all German forces in Yugoslavia and Albania, was also Supreme Headquarters, Southeast. As Commander-in-Chief, Southeast, Marshal von Weichs controlled Army Group E as well, in effect placing Army Group F in the position of being the headquarters to which Army Group E was responsible.

As subordinate commands in Yugoslavia and Albania, Army Group F had the Second Panzer Army, with headquarters at Kragujevac, and the Military Command, Southeast, with headquarters at Belgrade. Actually, the titles of both headquarters were inaccurate, since the Second Panzer Army had no armored divisions at the time and but one or two tank battalions as army troops, while the Military Commander, Southeast, was the area commander in Serbia, and commanded the tactical troops in the area in the dual role of Army Commander, Serbia. Although the Second Panzer Army retained its designation until the end, it might have been more properly called the Second Mountain Army. Attached to these two commands and Army Group F were the I Bulgarian Corps of four divisions; four German corps, with eleven infantry, one cavalry (Cossack), one mountain, and one SS mountain division; and army and army group troops.

Facing a better-armed and more numerous enemy than the German forces in Greece, Army Group F was all but forced on the defensive in the opening months of 1944. While the Chetniks still maintained an uneasy peace, the Partisans had grown to a force able to hold a large area of the country by themselves, including even transportation and communications facilities, and to set up a provisional government. Small-scale operations by the various divisions and smaller units met with some success, but the center of the Partisan movement, in the Knin-Jajce-Bihac-Banja Luka area, remained a refuge to which Tito's units could withdraw when German pressure became too great in any other particular area. (Map 3) Accordingly, to regain the initiative now all but lost, and to strike the Partisans a blow from which they would not soon recover, Marshal von Weichs ordered the Second Panzer Army to destroy the Tito forces in their main stronghold. The operation was known as ROESSELSPRUNG, and it was planned to commit elements of the 1st Mountain Division, elements of the Division Brandenburg (designation of a special demolitions and sabotage unit), the 202d Tank Battalion, the 92d Motorized Infantry Regiment (Separate), an SS parachute battalion, and a number of Croatian units.

The parachutists and glider troops were dropped on Tito's headquarters at Dvar on 25 May, while tank and infantry units converged from Bihac, Banja Luka, and Livno. Though Tito himself managed to escape, the Partisan headquarters was captured, with its extensive communications system. The 1st and 6th Partisan Divisions were badly mauled in the fighting, suffering a total of 6,000 casualties, and an enormous stock of booty taken. Though not a fatal blow, the operation did achieve its purpose in that the Partisan chain of command was temporarily broken until Tito could establish himself on the island of Vis under British protection, and the heavy personnel and materiel losses forced the guerrillas to withdraw from operations in the area to reorganize and regroup. The German satisfaction over the results of the operation was somewhat tempered, however, with the losses inflicted on the attackers when United States and British aircraft surprised them in the process of combing and clearing the Hvar area.

Strong concentrations of Partisans in Montenegro made it necessary to plan another large-scale operation, called RUEBEZAHL. However, before RUEBEZAHL could be launched, the movement of Partisans toward the Macedonia region required immediate and effective action. Aware of the impending German withdrawal from Greece and the Soviet advance to the west, the Partisans rushed the first of an estimated thirteen divisions in the direction of the strategic area north of Skoplje. Operation ROESLEIN cost the attackers almost a thousand casualties, but could not prevent a strong force from seizing a stretch of the highway north of Skoplje on 2 August; a hastily formed task force, with a reconnaissance battalion as its nucleus, managed to drive the Partisans off after heavy fighting. To the north, Operation FEUERWEHR inflicted more casualties on the Partisans, but could not prevent their movement into the upper valley of the Morava River.

On 12 August Operation RUEBEZAHL finally got underway, with the 1st Mountain Division and other German forces holding the major part of the advancing Partisan divisions and then driving them back across the Lim River. The results of the operation, though satisfactory in that the Partisans had been stopped from moving into Macedonia in force, were limited by the lack of a German parachute battalion, prevented by a shortage of gasoline from participating in the undertaking in its normal role. Also, the worsening situation with the Bulgarians and Romanians caused the German command to withdraw the 1st Mountain Division as soon as the operation had been completed, preventing exploitation of its success. Too, Partisan units that had managed to move to the east were now in position to threaten all road and rail transportation to the north and Belgrade. (Map 6.)

On 20 August the Russians launched a drive deep into Romania, and on 24 August another of Germany's allies went the way of the Italians a year earlier. The German military headquarters in Bucha-

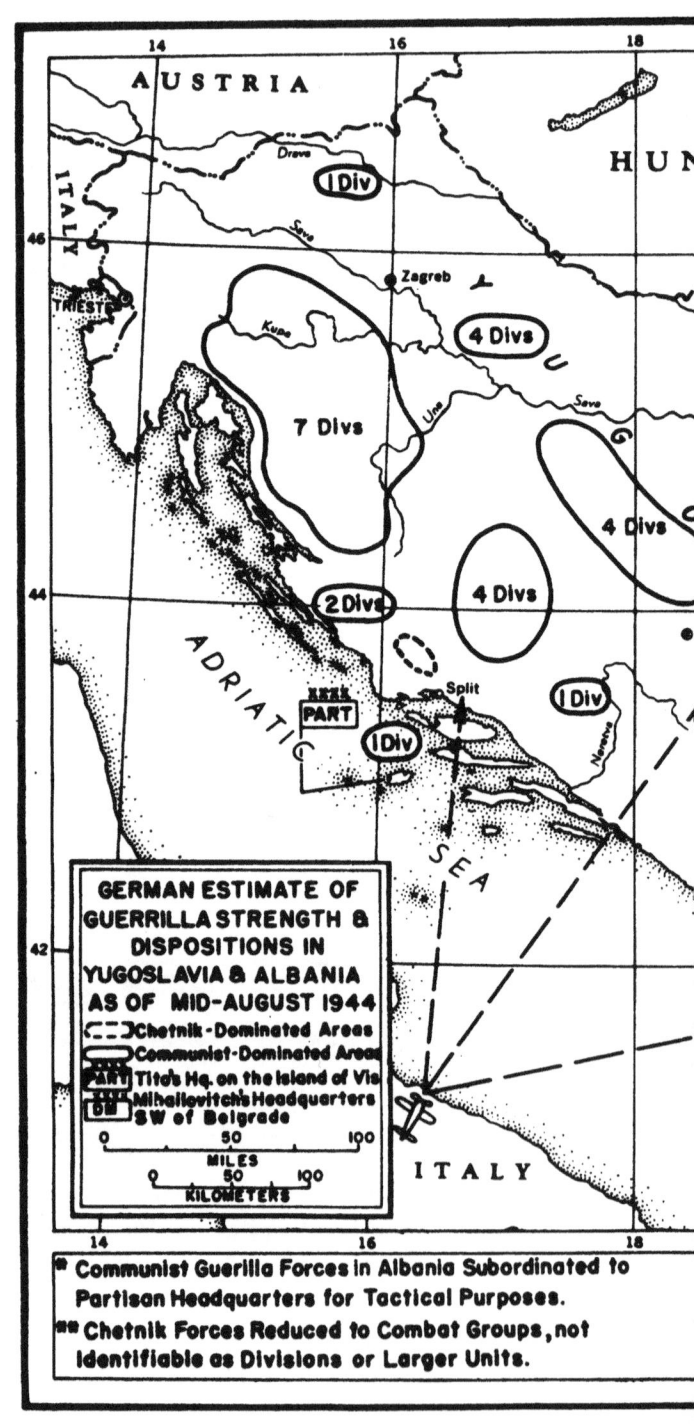

MAP 6.—German estimate of guerrilla strength and dispo

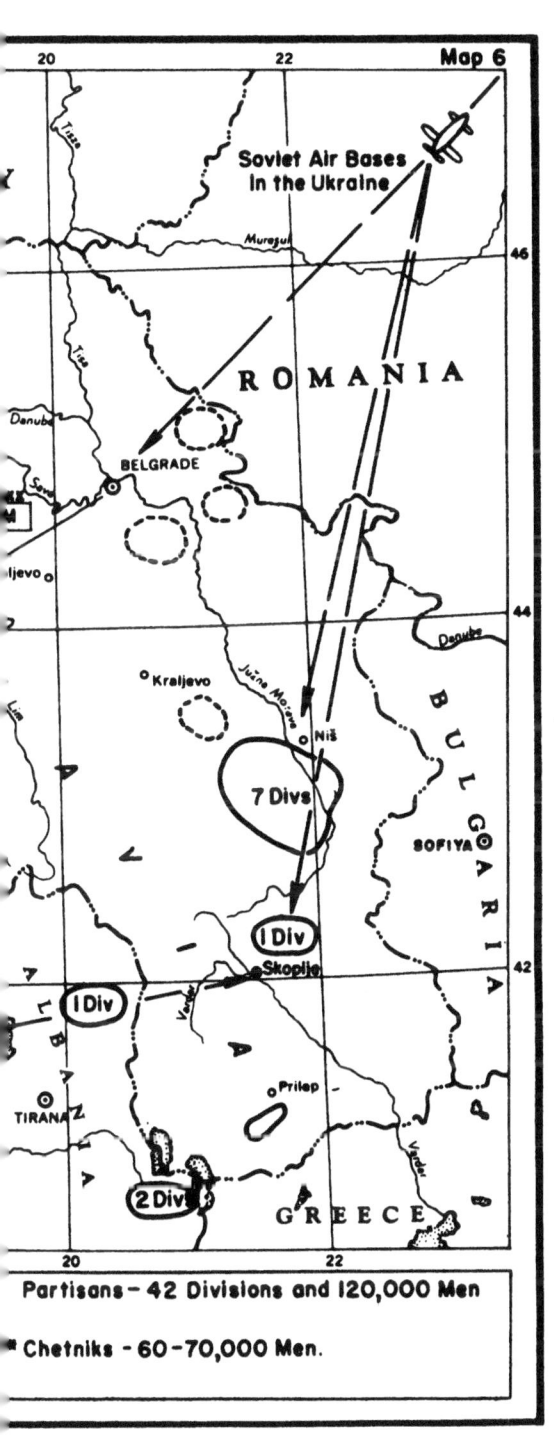

...oslavia and Albania as of mid-August 1944.

rest was invested by Romanian troops, and tank units had to be rushed to its relief. A few days later, Romanian troops joined Soviet forces in a campaign to drive the Germans out of Romania. The Bulgarians, meanwhile, had begun to assemble their occupation units in Macedonia into a compact force in the area just west of their own national border.

On 8 September, Bulgaria was at war with Germany and the Bulgarian I Corps was already in contact with the Partisan forces that had managed to infiltrate east to the Morava. Awaiting heavy Soviet and Bulgarian reinforcements from the Sofiya area, the I Corps held in place. Farther south, the V Corps was in defensive positions east of Skoplje, though units in and about the city itself put up a stubborn struggle against the 1st Mountain Division on its arrival in TREU-BRUCH. North of Skoplje, the 2d, 5th, and 17th Divisions of the Partisan II Corps had been identified. Immediately engaging both Bulgarians and Partisans, the 1st Mountain Division cleared the main routes to the north and secured the city of Skoplje itself. However, the division lacked the strength to destroy the guerrilla and Bulgarian forces or to drive them from the area.

It is important to note, at this point, that the Germans had begun to use the Partisan and other guerrilla designations for the irregular units. Before this time, the usual reference in German reports had been to "bands." But from mid-1944, operations orders and the war diaries of the German units committed against the guerrillas began to carry the guerrilla forces as brigades, divisions, and corps, with numerical designation when known. In a conference on 21 September, Marshal von Weichs expressed the view that the size, armament, organization, and operations of the Partisan units justified the Germans' considering them as an enemy on the same plane with the regular forces of the other nations with which the Reich was at war.

To keep the various small units and administrative detachments scattered over Yugoslavia intact while the fighting to secure the Skoplje area was in progress, Army Group F directed their concentration in central locations and the organization of an all-round defense. All female personnel were ordered evacuated, and plans drawn up to destroy all supplies that could not be moved. Outlying garrisons were stripped of combat units to build up the mobile force assembling under Second Panzer Army in the area south of Belgrade.

After an appeal by Prime Minister Nedıtch, the Serbian State Guard and security units were issued additional ammunition. However, it was obviously already too late to strengthen either the Serbian auxiliaries or the demoralized Croatian Ustascha. The Chetniks, facing complete annihilation at the hands of the Partisans, rendered

CHART No. 4—GERMAN GROUND FORCES IN OCCUPIED YUGOSLAVIA AND ALBANIA AS OF THE FALL BELGRADE 20 OCTOBER 1944

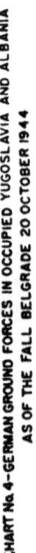

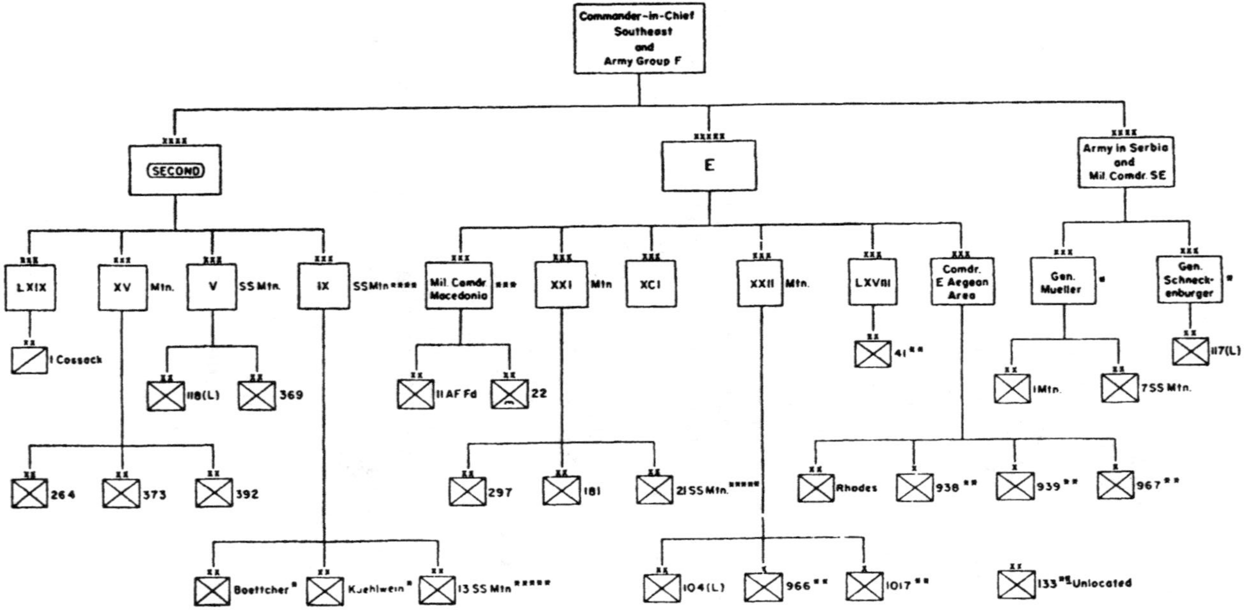

* Kampfgruppen (Battle Groups) Of Division Size Or Larger.

** Fortress Troops.

*** Formed To Coordinate Efforts Of Units Assigned To Holding Open Escape Route Of Army Group E From Greece To Area Of Serbia North Of Macedonia.

**** Formed In The Summer Of 1944 To Control Albanian And Croatian SS Divisions.

***** 13th SS Mountain Division (Handschar) Arrived In Slovenia In Early 1944. 21st SS Mountain Division (Skanderbeg) Was Formed In The Summer Of 1944 Of Albanian Personnel.

Chart 4.

some service in the capacity of security troops, but could not be depended upon not to attack small German detachments whenever the opportunity presented itself.

By late September Soviet forces were fighting north of Belgrade, in an encircling move to capture the city. The Second Panzer Army lacked the forces to implement German plans for an overpowering counterattack, and withdrew its weakened units into western Croatia. On the 27th of the month, Marshal von Weichs directed the impressment of all residents of Belgrade in the building of fortifications. However, threatened with encirclement, the command post of Army Group F had to be displaced to the north and west.

Belgrade fell to the Russians and the I Partisan Corps on 20 October. (Chart 4.) In the south, the rear guard of the German forces was approaching the Greek-Yugoslav frontier, leaving Greece in the hands of ELAS, EDES, and the British. Still in good order, the units of Army Groups E and F made their way to the northwest, keeping open secondary rail and road lines to evacuate the last of their forces from Macedonia, Albania, and Montenegro. Thousands of Chetniks, Serb auxiliaries, Croatian soldiers, and individuals who had assisted the occupation forces in one way or another joined the columns of withdrawing German troops.

The guerrilla movement at this point can be considered at an end. The resistance forces, with the assistance of the Allies and aided by the worsening German strategic situation, had finally been able to emerge as an organized force, be recognized as such by the Germans, and contribute materially to the liberation of their respective countries. In turn, these resistance forces had speeded the breaking of German power by tying down well over one-half million German troops and preventing their commitment on other fronts. In Yugoslavia, Tito was to become de-facto chief of state and crush his Chetnik opponents; in Albania, civil war was to ensue until Enver Hoxha and his communist faction could seize control of the country. With the military operations shifting to the north and west, the hinterlands of Albania and Yugoslavia and a large part of Greece became the scene of even more savage fighting as the communists made their ruthless bid for power.

CHAPTER 11

GEMSBOCK AND STEINADLER

Two large-scale operations in mid-1944, one conducted in northern Greece and southern Albania, the other in northern Greece, may be considered as typical of Balkan antiguerrilla warfare. The terrain over which the operations were conducted was ideal for irregulars, with high and rugged mountains paralleling the roads vital to the extended supply lines of the occupation forces. The tactics used in both operations, surrounding the enemy forces and then narrowing and closing the circle, were the most effective means devised by the Germans for fighting guerrillas. Lastly, the guerrillas were fighting over terrain they knew well, an advantage balanced by the superior fire power of the Germans.

GEMSBOCK took place between 6 and 14 June, with the 1st Mountain and 297th Infantry Divisions, and the Division Group (Provisional Division) Steyrer, composed of a number of security battalions, participating. (Map 7.) The 1st Mountain Division, as the strongest and most experienced, held the widest front, extending from Gramsh in the north, through Korca, to Vasilikon in the south. The 297th Infantry Division, in turn, held the line from a point west of Gramsh to Valona. On the south, Division Group Steyrer held the front from a point west of Vasilikon to the sea at Sarande. The XXII Mountain Corps, directing the operation, had its command post at Vasilikon and the mission of destroying an estimated 9,000 ELAS and other communist irregulars in the rough square within the line Korca-Valona-Sarande-Vasilikon. The final assembly areas, to be occupied just before the attack, were situated as far as possible from the communist headquarters at Corovda, in order to prevent outlying guerrilla groups from escaping.

Despite detailed planning, the first phase of the operation was a risk in that each man had to cover a front of over 100 yards. It was of the utmost importance, therefore, that enemy intentions to effect a breakout be determined as soon as possible; this disadvantage would decrease as the circle was compressed.

A shortage of fuel delayed the 297th Infantry Division in its movement to assembly areas, allowing the guerrillas time to collect their scattered units and devise a plan of defense. With the operation finally under way, heavy fighting developed on the front of the 1st

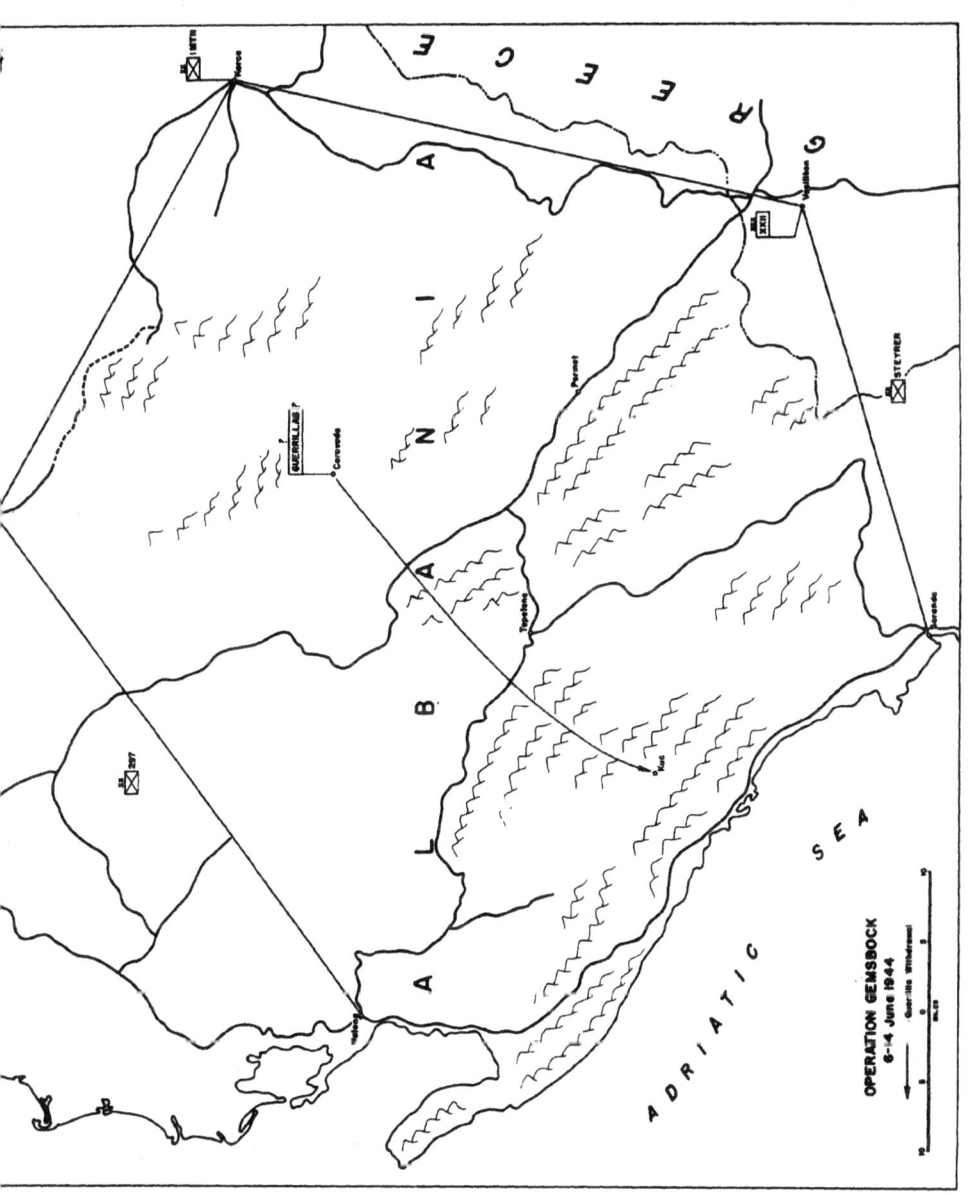

MAP 7.—Operations GEMSBOCK.

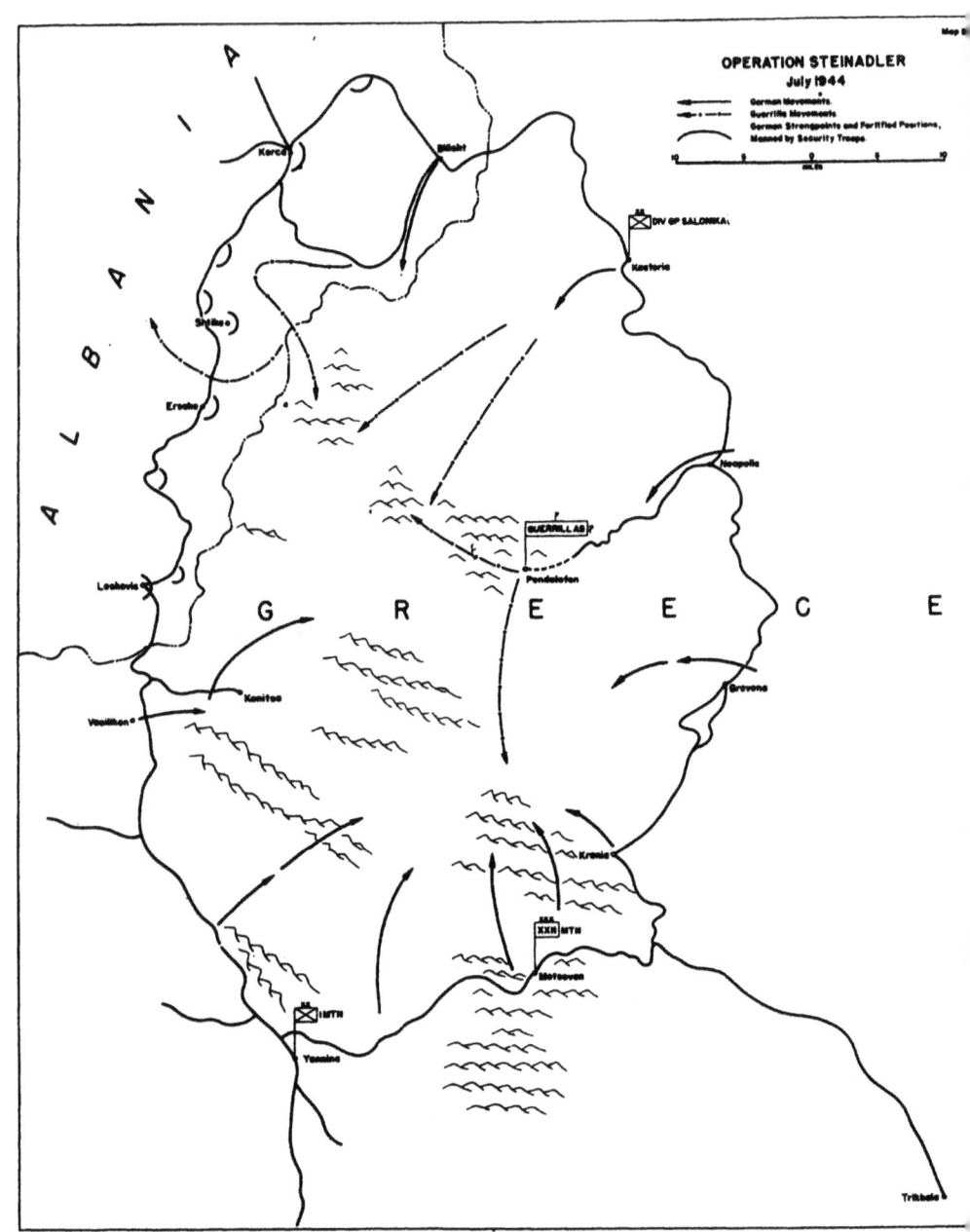

MAP 8.—Operation STEINADLER.

Mountain Division, which succeeded in driving the guerrillas before it as the division moved westward. Probing for gaps in the German front, a number of small guerrilla groups slipped through the line formed by the 297th Infantry Division and fled to the north; the remainder of the guerrilla force moved southward, into a stronghold west of the road Vasilikon–Permet–Tepelene.

Reaching the road on the fourth day of the operation, the mountain division rested and regrouped to climb the almost vertical slopes west of Permet the following morning. With escape to the north and south now blocked off, the remaining guerrillas were compressed into the mountain area about Kuc and eliminated in another three days of hard fighting. The terrain, honeycombed with caves, had to be searched carefully and the guerrillas had to be killed or captured in hand-to-hand fighting.

GEMSBOCK cost the guerrillas over 2,500 dead and prisoners, and a large stock of arms; German casualties for the operation were 120 killed and 300 wounded.

Three weeks after the close of GEMSBOCK, the XXII Mountain Corps took the field in Operation STEINADLER, to destroy the guerrilla forces threatening the Korca–Yannina and Yannina–Trikkala roads. (Map 8.) Attached to the corps for the operation were the 1st Mountain Division, a provisional division formed from elements of the Corps Group Salonika, and a number of security battalions. Estimates of the enemy strength were vague, but could probably be put at 6,000–8,000. Of considerable significance was the close liaison between these Greek guerrillas and the strong communist groups in Albania just across the frontier.

As a security measure, only the minimum number of commanders and staff officers were informed of the operational plan, while the troops were told they were assembling for a series of small-scale operations. Further steps to preserve the secrecy of the operation consisted of radio silence on the part of units moving into the area, small-scale troop movements in adjacent areas, and radio traffic from the light division below Arta indicating an attack farther south. The radio net operated by the guerrillas was monitored carefully to determine their reaction to these measures and to detect possible alerting of their units. Air reconnaissance was extended into Albania in order to allay guerrilla suspicions over unusual interest in the area.

Setting up its command post in the vicinity of Metsovan, the XXII Mountain Corps deployed the 1st Mountain Division along a line extending from that point to Yannina, Vasilikon, and Leskovic. Strongpoints and reinforced security units acting as a blocking force secured the road from Leskovic to the north and a junction with the Salonika Division Group near Korca. From a point east of Korca, the Salonika force was responsible for the line Bilisht-Kastoria-Neapolis-Grevena-Krania-Metsovan.

Aware of their predicament as soon as the German troops had detrucked, the guerrillas evacuated Pendalofon and moved into the mountains. Air reconnaissance reported them still within the encirclement, however, and the troops continued their movement as planned. The first day ended with elements of the 1st Mountain Division held up by stiff resistance north of Metsovan. During the day, troops of the Salonika Division Group repulsed an attempt by a strong guerrilla force to break out at Grevena.

On the second day, the Salonika Division Group was forced to halt and reorganize, having found it difficult to maintain cohesion over the rough terrain. The 1st Mountain Division, meanwhile, became heavily engaged at close quarters when it attempted to break through the resistance to its front. It was in this engagement that a battalion aid station, moved too far forward, was overrun by the guerrillas and eighty wounded were murdered and mutilated.

On its left, the 1st Mountain Division managed to forge ahead and on the third day enveloped the guerrilla pocket north of Metsovan, only to find a large part of the defending force had escaped to the northwest. Some 1,500 guerrillas were compressed in a ring about Pendalofon and destroyed in a systematic combing operation lasting two more days.

STEINADLER cost the Greek guerrillas a total of 567 dead and 976 prisoners. In addition, 341 Italians and seven Britons were also captured. The booty taken included 10 tons of explosives, over three quarters of a million rounds of rifle and machinegun ammunition, and 10,000 head of livestock, mostly sheep and goats. Despite these losses, the guerrilla forces began to regroup as soon as the German combat troops had left the area.

PART FOUR
RESULTS AND CONCLUSIONS

A compilation of casualties sustained by the combatants in the Balkans during the period of the occupation would not present a true picture of the enormous loss in personnel and materiel, or of real property. Actually, operations in that area during the period from April of 1941 to the end of hostilities were a series of struggles within the framework of a major war. A large number of casualties were suffered by both EDES and ELAS in their intermittent conflicts and in the civil war that followed the German withdrawal. The same was also true of Yugoslavia, where Chetniks and Partisans fought one another and the Germans at the same time. The Yugoslav casualties were further compounded by the Croat-Serb strife, and the massacre of Serbs by the Ustascha, which occurred shortly after the establishment of the Croatian state. In Albania, the struggle between the nationalist and communist factions was no less bitter than the fight of both against the Italians and later the Germans.

In addition to the conflicts between nationalities within the same state and strife between political factions, there was also a determined attempt on the part of Serb Orthodox adherents of Mihailovitch to destroy the Mohammedan minority in Yugoslavia. The Germans added fuel to the flames of this fire by enlisting numerous Mohammedans in their forces and using them as occupation troops.

Finally, the occupation troops were composed of Italians, Bulgarians, and Hungarians, as well as Germans, and numerous foreign legionaries. While the Bulgarians were under German command, in large part, the situation was somewhat different with the Italians in that German units on coastal defense and in Italian-occupied areas were often under Italian command. Of the legionaries, some, such as the Russian Guard Corps, were integrated into the Wehrmacht, while others, for example the Serbian State Guard, were not. While the losses of the Russian Guard Corps would be counted among the German casualties, the personnel of the Serbian State Guard killed, wounded, and missing would not be, despite the fact they may have been fighting side by side.

Finally, German casualties from disease, chiefly typhoid, dysentery, and malaria, were unusually high, as were losses from direct physical exhaustion in the long marches and movements over rough terrain. The majority of the German personnel throughout the operations were of the older age groups and, except for the mountain units, had had little or no experience or conditioning for the type of warfare in which they had to engage.

On the basis of incomplete casualty figures, it can be said with some degree of accuracy that 1 out of 7 soldiers in German uniform, whether German or not, became a casualty by the close of operations. At the time of the capitulation, thousands more fell into Yugoslav hands, when they did not manage to get clear of the Balkans to surrender to Allied forces in Italy or Austria.

All three occupied countries were impoverished by the peninsula-wide fighting and reprisals. Greece, a maritime country, lost the bulk of the merchant fleet upon which it depended for its very existence. Yugoslavia, a grain-producing country that supplied food to much of southern Europe, could no longer even feed itself. Albania, the least developed of the three, lost a large part of the livestock upon which the national economy was based. In a 1-month period in mid-1944, a full quarter of all the locomotives in the Balkans were destroyed by Allied air attacks, a most serious loss in view of the inadequate road system and uneven distribution of food-producing areas. In Yugoslavia, the facilities of numerous mines were destroyed by sabotage, in the fighting to retake them, or demolished by the withdrawing occupation forces.

Perhaps the most significant results of the occupation were in the political field. Two kingdoms fell, if Albania is considered, and replaced by communist dictatorships; Greece was prevented from sharing their fate only by the prompt intervention of strong British ground forces, supported by air and naval units. As was to be expected, the assumption of power by the communists was followed shortly by the elimination of all political opposition and the establishment of one-party states.

The successes achieved by the guerrillas against the Germans, Italians, and Bulgarians in the Balkans during World War II strengthened considerably the tradition of resistance to foreign occupation forces. Communist indoctrination of large segments of the population, with stress placed on clandestine methods and guerrilla tactics, also played its part in awakening this sentiment. Thus there is little doubt that a foreign invader today, whether from East or West, would be confronted with a formidable task of pacification following a successful campaign against the regular forces of the Balkan nations.

The experience of the Germans in their Balkan occupation also offers a number of lessons in the administration of conquered enemy countries and is a measure of what a future occupier might expect in that area. Before launching into a consideration of the sound as well as the injudicious aspects of the German occupation proper, however, it might be well to visualize the situation in which the Wehrmacht found itself in relation to its allies in Greece and Yugoslavia following the surrender of those two countries.

Regarded as the chief architect of their defeat by the Greeks, the Wehrmacht turned over the bulk of the occupation responsibility to the Italians in 1941. Already smarting under defeats in Africa at the hands of the British and having made a poor showing in their own Balkan campaigns, the Italians undertook no appreciable measures to prevent the growth of a guerrilla movement. The few Italian attempts at suppression, harsh and arbitrary, only kindled the resentment of the Greek population and placed a further onus on the Germans. Even more resented was the German invitation to the Bulgarians to annex Thrace, won at the cost of so many thousands of Greek lives in 1922-24 and still fresh in the minds of the bulk of the Greek population.

Yugoslavia, to appease Italian, Bulgarian, and Hungarian ambitions, was partitioned and temporarily ceased to exist as a sovereign state. Even worse, one large minority, the Croats, were granted their independence and then accepted into the ranks of the German satellites. Italian and Bulgarian reprisals for guerrilla activities, often inflicted on the innocent, alienated still more the bulk of the population, which also attributed the excess of the Croat Ustascha to the Germans as well as the Italians.

In their own zones of the occupied countries, the Germans exploited the economy for as much as it could bear, leaving the civilian population at a scant subsistence level and in many cases at a level so low that the relief agencies of neutral powers had to be called upon to prevent widespread starvation. This, the raising of native collaborationist forces to augment their own, and the obvious fact that there would be no relief so long as the Germans remained, placed the occupiers in a position that could only be held with increasing force as time passed.

Shorn of allies by the defection of the Italians and Bulgarians, the Germans found themselves in possession of a rugged and largely mountain area seething with discontent, where even former collaborators were eager to join the winning side, well exemplified in the cases of EDES and a number of the Chetnik units.

In brief, this multinational suppression of the heterogeneous peoples of several national states was doomed to failure by the lack of central direction and the divergent aims of the Germans, Italians, and Bulgarians. Had one power alone administered the occupation and held out some hope of eventual relief to the conquered nations, better results might well have been achieved.

The system of parallel commands did not cease at the national level, in the German case, but extended down to the smallest units. While the Army, on the one side, was responsible to the Armed Forces High Command for the security of the Balkans, the SS was answerable to Himmler and his SS representatives except when engaged in field operations. Until the situation became critical and Marshal von Weichs was forced to assert his authority, SS units on occasion operated without Army control even in the field, and would cooperate in antiguerrilla operations only when it suited the individual commander and higher SS headquarters. Understandably, there was also considerable confusion and wasted effort in the operational and particularly in the clandestine intelligence field, with Wehrmacht and SS agencies trying to accomplish similar missions for their respective commands. This situation was further complicated by the activities of the German Foreign Office, which maintained its own version of a High Commissioner and was heavily staffed with personnel to accomplish political aims not always consonant with the directives given the military commanders. A single supreme authority representing the Reich, with clearly defined responsibilities, would have prevented much needless friction and waste of effort.

The German shortage of manpower reduced the forces made available for the Balkan occupation to the over-age and the physically limited, with the exception of a few units such as the 1st Mountain Division. Other measures taken to alleviate the manpower shortage were the employment of native troops and enlistment of foreign legionnaries, chiefly Russians and Caucasus Mountains peoples. While the first group was capable of but limited service, the other was considered not completely reliable and requiring close supervision by German officers and noncommissioned officers. In either case, the conduct of operations was limited to their restricted capabilities and extended pursuit of routed guerrilla forces was generally unsatisfactory. Moreover, the equipment, particularly armored and motor vehicles, was below the general Wehrmacht standard and resulted in numerous breakdowns that might otherwise not have occurred. Motor parts alone kept vehicles deadlined for extended periods of time, until similar vehicles could be cannibalized and a reduced number of trucks, armored cars, and tanks could again be put into operating condition. Both personnel and vehicle situations were made unavoidable by the heavy demands of the active theaters of war, but it can be presumed that with personnel fit for full field service, properly equipped and mounted in more serviceable vehicles, fewer men would have been necessary to maintain order, and the results of operations would have been more satisfactory.

The German occupiers were very much aware of the importance of security measures required in their situation. Yet it is quite apparent that such measures were not adequate and seldom enforced. One feature of this laxity may be seen in the large numbers of local civilians hired to work in German troop areas and military installations. With only a most cursory security investigation, these Yugoslavs and Greeks had access to areas in which they could observe troop movements and preparations preceding operations, storage facilities for such sensitive items as gasoline and ammunition, and routine measures for defense. Since these civilians were paid by their own governments and presented no burden to the Germans, already overtaxed to provide personnel for operations, it is not too surprising that the occupiers took advantage of the opportunity to secure a large labor force. However, this convenience was more than offset by the compromise of almost every antiguerrilla operation of significance.

Commanders were reluctant to separate the troops from the civilian population entirely, both for morale reasons and in conformance with the German policy of exploiting the conquered countries even to the extent of having the troops buy up consumer goods for shipment home. This made unavoidable still more violations of security. In substance, the policy of the Germans toward the outwardly cooperative portion of the population was far more lenient than security demanded.

The German tendency to underestimate the guerrillas also played its part in the undermining of the occupation. At first, commanders felt the suppression of the guerrillas to be a function of the police. Later, when it became obvious the police could not restore order, the military commanders were forced to take the field. However, even after guerrilla activities had turned the Balkans into a theater of war, only intelligence reports carried the designations of guerilla units; commanders still referred to these forces in their headquarters diaries as "bands." Not until 1944, when the guerrillas were threatening to drive him from the Balkans altogether, did Marshal von Weichs acknowledge their strength and direct that reference be made to the guerrilla units as divisions, corps and other designations, rather than as "bands." Too, many of the demolitions and other technical operations of the guerrillas were ineffective and aroused the contempt of the Germans, but these were offset by their great number and the total amount of damage done.

A feature of significance but one over which the Germans could exercise little influence was the nature of the Balkan peoples themselves. Composed of hardy Greeks and Slavs, traditionally opposed to any occupier, they readily took up arms when it became apparent the conquerors intended to remain and to exploit their few resources; even the collaborationists often proved to be unreliable. Once started, the surge of the guerrilla movement could not be stopped even by the wholesale slaughter of hostages.

It is unlikely that German commanders will ever face these occupation problems in the Balkans again. However, a review of the mistakes these commanders made would undoubtedly cause them to urge any future occupier to begin his administration with a clear-cut statement of policy, including a promise of eventual withdrawal of occupation troops and self-determination for the people; a unified military command and distinct delineation of responsibility in the political and military fields; the assignment of trained, well-equipped combat troops in adequate numbers to the area; the taking of prompt and effective though not excessively harsh measures to quell disorders; and an extensive propaganda campaign to explain the purpose of the occupation and the benefits to accrue to the population with the maintenance of law and order. Finally, they would most certainly recommend the troops be supplied from outside the country and restrained from excesses. With perseverance, the occupation forces might then be able to avoid the Balkan chaos of 1941–44.

APPENDIX I
CHRONOLOGY OF EVENTS

1940
October 1940
- 28. Italian forces attack Greece from Albania.

1941
April 1941
- 3 Rommel opens his offensive in Libya.
- 6 German forces intervene in the Greek-Italian conflict.
- 6 German troops invade Yugoslavia.
- 17 Yugoslav High Command forced to capitulate.
- 20 General Tsolakoglou surrenders the Army of Epirus to the Germans.
- 23 Greece surrenders to the Germans and Italians.
- 27 German troops enter Athens.

May 1941
- 29 Rommel stopped at the Egyptian frontier.

June 1941
- 9 Field Marshal List, commander of Twelfth Army, appointed Armed Forces Commander, Southeast.
- 22 Operation BARBAROSSA begins.
- late Bulk of German combat troops shifted from Balkans to Russian theater; number of sabotage incidents in Balkans increases.

July 1941
- 13 Inhabitants of Montenegro launch general attack on scattered Italian garrisons.

August 1941
- Early Italian army headquarters redesignated area commands.
- Tito moves his headquarters into the field.
- Daily attacks on Serbian police stations.

September 1941
- 5 WB Southeast transfers 125th Infantry Regiment (Separate) from Salonika area to Belgrade.
- 16 Hitler issues directive ordering Marshal List to suppress revolt in Balkans.

October 1941
- 25 Marshal List relinquishes duties because of illness; General Kuntze appointed acting Armed Forces Commander, Southeast.
- 27 Headquarters, Twelfth Army (Armed Forces Commander, Southeast) moves from Athens to Salonika.

December 1941
- 11 Germany and Italy declare war on the United States.

1942

January 1942
- 15–26 Major antiguerrilla operations in Croatia.
- 18 Second British drive into Libya stopped.

March 1942
- 1 Headquarters, LXV Corps Command and headquarters, Military Command, Serbia, merged.

April–May 1942
- 20 April–3 May First major joint antiguerrilla operation launched by Italian, German, and Croatian troops.

May 1942
- 27 Rommel opens second drive into Egypt.

July 1942
- General Robotti launches drive on Partisans in Slovenia.
- Total Yugoslavia guerrilla losses to date estimated at 45,000 dead.

August 1942
- 8 General Kuntze relieved by General Loehr as Armed Forces Commander, Southeast.

October 1942
- 23 Start of the Battle of El Alamein.

November 1942
- 8 Allies invade North Africa.
- 19 Russians launch Stalingrad counteroffensive.
- 25 Guerillas blow up Gorgopotamos Bridge, some 100 miles north of Athens.

December 1942
- 28 Hitler issues directive raising status of Armed Forces Commander, Southeast, to that of Commander-in-Chief, Southeast.

1943

May 1943
- 8–12 End of Axis resistance in North Africa.

June 1943
- EDES ceases active operations against Germans.

July 1943
- 10 Allies establish lodgment in Sicily.
- 25 Mussolini forced to resign.
- 26 Directive No. 48 introduces major organizational changes and centralizes authority for defense of the Balkan Peninsula. Field Marshal von Weichs named new Commander-in-Chief, Southeast.

August 1943
- 18 Resistance in Sicily collapses.

September 1943
- 2 Allies land in southern Italy.
- 3 Italy signs armistice.

September 1943
- 17 Allies capture Foggia air base.
- 19 Armed Forces High Command directive makes Rommel and Army Group B responsible for destroying guerilla forces in Istria.
- end German forces in Balkans total 600,000 men.

October 1943
- 1 Allies land at Salerno.

1943—Continued

November 1943
- 17   British and Italian garrison of Leros surrenders to the Germans

1944

January 1944
- 22   Allies land at Anzio.

March 1944
- 26   Russian troops reach the Romanian border.

May 1944
- 25   German airborne troops attack Tito's headquarters at Dvar.

June 1944
- 4   Allied troops enter Rome.
- 6   Invasion of Normandy.
- 6–14   Operation GEMSBOCK.

July 1944
- 3   EDES reopens hostilities.
- 5–6   EDES forces attack German troops near Arta.
- Beginning   Operation STEINADLER launched.

August 1944
- 2   Partisans advance into Macedonia.

August 1944
- 5   Operation KREUZOTTER begins.
- 12   Operation RUEBEZAHL gets under way.
- 12   Florence captured by the Allies after heavy fighting.
- 20   Russians launch deep drive into Romania.
- 24   Romanian Government surrenders to the Soviet Union.

September 1944
- 5   Soviet Union declares war on Bulgaria.
- 8   Bulgaria asks Russians for armistice and declares war on Germany.
- 8–9   General rising takes place in southern and central Greece.
- 12   United States First Army crosses the German frontier.
- 21   Marshal von Weichs considers Partisan units as equivalent to regular forces.
- late   Russians fighting north of Belgrade.

October 1944
- 12   26,500 Germans still stranded on Crete, Rhodes, and other islands.
- 14   Army Group E headquarters moves to Macedonia.
- 20   Belgrade falls to the Russians and the I Partisan Corps.

November 1944
- 2   Last German units evacuate Greece.

APPENDIX II
BIBLIOGRAPHICAL NOTE

The German official sources used in the preparation of this study included the war diaries (*Kriegstagebuecher*) of the Commander-in-Chief and Armed Forces Commander, Southeast; of Army Groups E and F; of the territorial commanders (*Militaerbefehlshaber*) in Serbia and southern Greece, and such selected corps and division diaries as were available. In addition to these, reference was made to those portions of the war diaries of the Armed Forces High Command and Armed Forces Operations Staff (*Wehrmachtfuehrungsstab*), and such Hitler Directives (*Fuehrerweisungen*) as applied to the southeastern theater.

Other official sources such as résumés of the conferences of senior commanders and staffs included in the headquarters files, summaries of operations such as "The Great Withdrawal in the Southeast" (*Die Grosse Absetzbewegung im Suedosten*), and various activity reports supplemented the chronological record of events presented in the diaries.

A personal touch was added to the official record by the eyewitness accounts of General Lanz in his "Guerrilla War in the Mountains" and Colonel Gaisser in his "Guerrilla Battles in Croatia."[1] Similar material, from a more detached viewpoint, was found in various commentaries by General der Artillerie (Lieutenant General) Walter Warlimont, Deputy Chief of the Armed Forces Operations Staff. Reference was made to unofficial German publications and non-German sources, including the accounts of former Allied liaison officers, only where necessary to fill gaps in the official records and monographs.

---
[1] See foreword.

www.ingramcontent.com/pod-product-compliance
Lightning Source LLC
Chambersburg PA
CBHW070322100426
42743CB00011B/2515